I Know a Girl

Amy Sadd, Author

Copyright © 2025
All rights reserved.

Published by Mi Princesa Publishing

This book is based on the memoirs of the author.

ISBN: 979-8-9999185-0-5 ebook

ISBN: 979-8-9999185-1-2 paperback

ISBN: 979-8-9999185-2-9 paperback wide release

QUANTITY PURCHASES for schools, companies, organizations, clubs, groups may be arranged at a discount by contacting the publisher.

Early Reviews:

My bedtime is 9 pm: Here it is 10:30 and I keep telling myself just one more story! *R.B*

I thought I knew Amy. Comes to find out; after reading her book, I never knew one person could keep going and help so many others after so much loss. *L.H*

I Know a Girl hit me the same way as the book *WILD,* but without the hiking. Which is great because I do not hike. Really great read in small chapters to take with you. *J.C.*

In *I Know a Girl*, Amy Sadd writes of her abuse, trauma, and devastating losses (including infant loss and surviving suicide attempts) with raw unflinching honesty. With raw truth and unexpected beauty, Amy shares how trauma, grief, and survival shaped her and how family, both found and rediscovered, gave her a place to belong. This memoir isn't neat redemption; it's the messy, luminous path of staying alive and finding meaning where no one expected it. *S.A.H.*

I Know a Girl speaks of such things that most people do not have to live through. Amy is the epitome of what I call strong. She put her heart and soul out there for the world to see and I think that is very very brave. In life, people don't always tell the hard stories of what they have been through. Most are too ashamed, scared, or not able to. She puts it out there for all of us to not only read but to try to understand another person's story that isn't pretty but is real, honest, raw and emotionally riveting. I was lucky enough to be able to ARC read this for her and I am very honored that she entrusted me with her story. Everyone needs to read this story. You will finish it with a changed perspective on other people's trauma. -*D.H.*

This memoir captured my heart. Amy writes with such honesty and vulnerability that you can feel each word. Her story is raw, gut wrenching, brave. But most importantly, human. This is a reminder that healing is not out of reach. This is a very powerful read. It's a story of resilience, hope, and finding light through the cracks. *D.A.*

A memoir that doesn't just tell a story, it gives you a piece of someone's soul. "I Know a Girl" by Amy Sadd is a memoir that is as brave as it is beautifully written. Amy opens up her life to the reader with honesty, vulnerability, and strength and it's impossible not to feel every word. This book is a reminder that our stories, even the painful ones, matter. Amy's voice is raw and authentic, and her willingness to share her journey makes this memoir not only impactful, but also deeply inspiring.

Reading this felt like being invited into someone's heart and handed a piece of their truth. It's the kind of memoir that stays with you long after you finish, urging you to reflect on your own story, resilience, and healing.

Vulnerable, powerful, and beautifully human. This book is a reminder that our stories matter. C.E

I Know a Girl by Amy Sadd broke me open and gently put the pieces back together. This memoir is raw, unfiltered, and deeply personal. I cried so much reading it because it felt like she was telling parts of my own story. Amy doesn't just survive-she fights, feels, and keeps moving forward with a quiet strength that's unforgettable. Her words are beautifully vulnerable, and her journey through trauma, loss, and healing is told with unflinching honesty and grace. I just wanted to reach into the pages and hug her. Her story isn't easy to read, but it's so important to witness. Every chapter feels like a quiet conversation over coffee with someone who's lived through hell and still found her way back to hope.

This isn't just a story of healing—it's messy, real, and incredibly moving. Amy's strength and openness let you feel every word. Her reflections on trauma, grief, and survival are powerful reminders that healing is possible and that your story matters too.

I highly recommend I Know a Girl to anyone navigating deep trauma, loss, or just needing a reminder that hope is still possible—even in the darkest places. -J.

About The Author

"Trauma tried to silence her. This book is how she found her voice."

Amy Sadd is a US Marine Corps Veteran, life coach, mother, grandmother, and memoirist whose works are shaped by resilience, faith, and her search for belonging. After surviving trauma, loss, and profound life transitions, she returned to school, earning her bachelor's degree in her mid-50's. She is currently pursuing her master's degree in psychology with an emphasis in Life Coaching.

Originally from Marina, California, and long periods in both Nebraska and Mississippi, Amy now makes her home on an island in Mexico. Her writing blends honesty with hope, exploring themes of healing, identity and cultural adaptation. Drawing from a life that spans military service, motherhood, academic achievement, and personal reinvention, Amy offers readers stories that are both deeply personal and universally human.

Amy Sadd writes unflinching memoirs of survival and renewal perfect for readers drawn to stories of hope after hardship.

When not writing, she can be found on her island, near the sea or in the jungle, reflecting on the past while imaging and creating new chapters of her life and work.

To My Girls:

I love you to the Moon and Back.

I see the Moon and the Moon sees you.

The Game. I Win.

I KNOW A GIRL

Memoir

Amy Sadd

Contents

Welcome

This book arises from the author's memories, experiences, and reflections. While rooted in real events, the stories are shaped by the passage of time and the nature of memory. Some names, identifying details, timelines, and circumstances have been altered, combined, or fictionalized to protect privacy, preserve dignity, and allow the narrative to flow.

The voices and perspectives presented here are the author's own, filtered through recollection, interpretation, and imagination. They are not meant to provide an objective record, but to convey a memoir of personal truth and meaning.

Readers should understand that if they recognize themselves or others in these pages, any resemblance may be partial, coincidental, or altered for narrative purposes. Some people are combined for ease of telling the story.

The intention is not to cause harm or misrepresentation, but to ***explore healing, growth, and resilience through storytelling.***

This book contains references to trauma, abuse, loss, and other sensitive experiences. These elements are part of the author's journey toward healing: They may be triggering for some readers.

Introduction

There are moments in life so sharp and so sweet that they settle into your bones and never leave.

Some of them hurt like hell. Some of them crack you wide open with laughter. Some of them come quietly, in the form of a boat you work on every day for months. Others come as Christmas spent handing out toys to other people's children and a different season spent serving at a Christmas soup kitchen. Those holidays showed me that giving is more healing and joyful than receiving ever could be. This book is filled with those moments: Stories of my life stitched together by survival, faith, stubbornness, and grace.

I didn't sit down to write this because I thought my story was extraordinary. I sat down because it wouldn't leave me alone. The memories knocked and pulled and tapped at my shoulder until I gave in and said, "Fine, let's talk." And once I started, I realized something powerful: I've been carrying a library inside me all along.

Some of these stories are about trauma, about being knocked down over and over again and somehow finding a way to stand, even to walk. Others are about the long, slow work of healing.

How to build a life after the storm, brick by brick, with shaking hands and a brave heart. It really does not matter if that storm is physical or emotional: they take the same steps to recovery. And many are about Cozumel, the place that adopted me when I wasn't sure I had anywhere to belong.

To my daughters, thank you. You were my first and only reason to try harder, to stand taller, to believe that even the most broken pieces of myself could be used for something good. You taught me to keep going, even when I didn't want to. You gave me the courage to write my truth. You gave me the strength to become the kind of woman who could keep going and try to be a better example when I really was not. Thank you for never giving up on me, even when I was not the mother you needed. Ultimately, you gave me the courage to live. This book is for you. *I am here today because of you*.

For anyone holding grief, terror, or fear in one hand and maybe only seeing a glimmer of hope in the other, may these pages remind you: There is still time. Still light. Still something waiting to be lived within you. For me it was something to be written.

Let's begin....

Prologue

How I learned who I was:

I was unwanted from conception.

I had heard the story over and over from as long as I remember:

My mother had been a few months pregnant and fell with one foot inside and one foot outside the bathtub and had miscarried. Two months later at the doctor she was shocked to find out she was still about 6 months pregnant. I was born at term in a very difficult birth. I was not her first child, so no complications were expected. However, at the last minute everything went wrong. I was stuck. When I was finally born, I was what they called at that time a "blue baby." I was not breathing. The oxygen in the room was broken. The delivery doctor pumped a manual oxygen mask by foot to no avail. He took me to another floor in the hospital to find a working oxygen mask and he is the one who finally gave me my first breath of life.

We left the hospital to live in a literal barn. We did not stay there long, but my single mother with 8 children did not have a lot of choice. She did her best, moving the family every few years into different low rent homes that had leaky roofs, unsealed and broken windows, and always in the wrong neighborhoods. We finally ended up in an apartment complex with hundreds of other poverty-stricken families, all trying to just survive.

My first abuser in my life was my mother. I slept with her in the same room in her double bed until I was 12 or 13. She more than often took her bad days out on me. She told me I was unwanted. I was a waste of oxygen. I should have died with my twin brother. I should not have survived my birth. I would never amount to anything. The words she told me shaped my inner being, my psyche and molded my life.

She often told people that I cried so much as an infant that she would tie me to my crib and take a walk. "Doctor's orders" she told people. She told others that I was a problem child as I got a little older.

"If I beat her once a month, that is enough to keep her in line."

That was her new mantra. When an infant and preschooler hears things and experiences abuse like this enough, those statements become the inner truth to the child for life.

I went to my first day of preschool, knowing the truths she taught me about myself. I was scared, confused and I did not have the nice clothes other kids had. All their moms and dads left them with hugs and kisses and promises to see them as soon as class was over. I was shoved through the door with no understanding of what was going on or why I was there.

The teachers were happily leading their morning welcome song:

"If you're happy and you know it, clap your hands..."

I was not happy, so I did not clap, stomp my feet, turn around or any of the other directions the song gave. At the end of the day the teacher asked my mother if I was ready for preschool, or maybe I needed more socializing.

That night I was beaten for not participating in class. From then on, I knew better than not to excel in whatever was put in front of me. As a tiny little 3-year-old girl, I realized that I was to perform perfectly in public.

At home I learned to be out of the way to avoid the inevitable violence. As we moved from house to house during my younger years, I always found a safe place. My own reading area and refuge: Under the table, on a stair landing, beside the couch near the front door. A tiny place of sanctuary where I could lose myself in book and dreams. A place I was close enough to hear her call for me, but out of the way of any blows that might land on the nearest child.

How the abuse of all her children was never discovered always made me wonder: Were we so unwanted and useless that no one would see what was happening and help us? Were we really that much trouble that no one cared to save us? Why did people laugh so hard when she told them she kept a beating belt in the diaper bag?

My only hope in those years was my favorite uncle who often spent time with me. In preschool and my early primary grades, and he would fix my hair and tell me I was pretty. I remember crying wishing it were true. Also, My eldest and second eldest brothers did what they could to protect me from the abuse when they were able. I tried to be with them as much as I was allowed.

But every single day, the night always came, and I was called to go to her bed. I was not to move until sunrise.

"Lay STILL and go to sleep." These words haunt me to this day.

I do not think she ever saw me as an individual human person. She only saw me as a burden. Anything that then happened to me, therefore, was also a burden:

I was sexually abused by a step grandfather for years. When I tried to tell at the age of 6, no one listened.

When I was raped at 12 by several adult black men in our apartment parking area. They told me white women were theirs to take for sex and that they would ruin me so that I did not deserve a true love. No one would want me, ever, since I was no longer a virgin. I told. But no one listened.

When I begged my father to come take me to his house in another state far away, he did not listen.

When I tried to report physical, emotional and mental abuse in my home to social workers in Nebraska at the age of 16, no one listened.

When I cried out for help and tried to commit suicide more than once as an adult, when I cried in counseling that I was in so much pain and turmoil internally that I know longer felt alive inside. No one listened.

The horrible things I was told, and believed about myself in those dark bedrooms, where I was not allowed to move for fear of being beaten again, followed me throughout my life.

I spent my entire life trying to overcome what I had learned and believed about who I was:

I am bad.

I do not deserve life.

I was and always will be unwanted.

I am ugly.

I am horrible.

I am not lovable.

I am unworthy of anything.

I did not deserve breath.

I should just die.

The Fewer, The Prouder, the Women Marines

At 18, I was lost. The day after my high school graduation, I was told to start paying the full pay the rent and utilities or leave.

I tried to go to community college to learn trade, but finances just did not work out in my favor. I was contemplating joining the military as two of my other siblings had done. It wasn't because I thought it would be glamorous, or I would become an instant hero in that beautiful uniform. It wasn't even about patriotism or glory. It wasn't about earning medals, uniforms, or parades. It was about survival. Joining the U.S. Marine Corps or Army would become my way to step out of poverty. I didn't go chasing honor. I went chasing stability. A paycheck. Maybe even a path to university, something I had always wanted but barely dared to imagine.

The day I signed that dotted line and chose the Marines, it also helped my older brother by giving him some extra time on leave to clear up a criminal charge. He would be rewarded with extra days of leave if he referred someone to the recruiter's office and they joined up under his name. I had not made a complete choice yet over Army or Marines, but that night it was made clear. When we were presented with this option, for my mother, the answer was easy: Join now and my brother would be ok. She never cared about what would happen to **me** or what I wanted.

Boot camp felt like an escape. I had three hot meals a day to fill my empty stomach, a warm bed to rest my tired body. Life had already thrown me more obstacles than I could count. It was just another challenge, but this time I knew what to expect and it was one I was ready to face.

The physical trials tested my every muscle, every ounce of my willpower. The first mornings were bitterly cold in January of 1988. Damp air sank into my bones before the sun had even risen, and my breath came in sharp bursts as I ran in formation. The cadence calls cut through the fog, boots pounding in perfect rhythm, the slap of soles on wet pavement sounding like one giant heartbeat. The metallic taste of sweat and sometimes blood from biting my lip to not cry out in pain filled my mouth, my muscles screaming. My hands blistered from rifle drills, the steel cold enough to bite through gloves, my shoulders aching from endless push-ups and mountain climbers in the sand pit until my arms shook uncontrollably. Sand fleas devoured us all.

One cold January morning in a South Carolina forest in training, I recalled surviving a particularly harsh freezing Nebraska winter. We were often without heat back then. My brother and I rose early, dressing and warming ourselves in front of the open oven, gulping hot chocolate or tea to warm our insides before a cold walk to high school. Looking back, it seems like 1930's not the 1980's. At least today, I knew eventually the Marines would take me back to where there was heat. I also had faith that the Drill Instructors would not actually let me die, even though they threatened otherwise often. Finally, someone to protect me and keep me safe.

But the physical trials weren't the hardest part as most Marines will agree. The real challenge was the mental battle: the voice that crept in when I was tired, my internal truths rising up telling me I wasn't strong enough, smart enough, worthy enough. These doubts were also driven into us daily. The Drill Instructors had a way of finding every crack in your particular armor. Sometimes, you'd get screamed at for doing something wrong; sometimes, for doing it right. It was a reminder of what I already knew from life — even when you follow every rule, you can still be told you're not enough.

I knew I had a mental advantage over some others. I had been yelled at and told I was told I was not good enough my entire life. That constant testing of worth and doubting one's ability at every turn was something I already knew well. I had been told "you're not enough" my whole life, the difference now was that I was learning to answer back without words, by doing what they said I couldn't.

I became the fastest runner on the entire platoon deck: Over 120 girls trying to become women. I enjoyed the freedom of just letting go, focusing only on my breath and the next step. There was no one who could take apart and reinstall the parts of an M 16 rifle faster than I. Platoon scribe? Yep, that was me, too, making sure everyone was accounted for if not in the squad bay. Sleepless night of rifle watch instilled a feeling of security I never had, knowing that when it was my turn to sleep, my sisters would have my back. No one could enter and hurt me in my sleep. The daily and weekly routines were something to believe and trust. For the first time in my life I felt as if the rug would not be pulled out from under me.

I will not lie to you or myself. There were moments of doubt that I felt I could not do it. In those moments I found something else inside me to look upon: a spark of resilience, a stubborn refusal to break. I kept going, not because I was sure I'd win, but because quitting wasn't an option anymore. If I did not finish boot camp, I would return to my hometown proving just what a failure I was. Life had already handed me hunger, instability, abuse and disappointment. I could not take another failure. The US Marine Corps was just another obstacle… except this time, I had chosen it. That experience planted a seed inside me, with the hope that maybe I could rewrite the story written for me in childhood by others.

Near the end of boot camp, our platoon was challenged by a male platoon to do the male obstacle course. The Female Drill Instructors wanted to prove that Women Marines were just as tough and capable as the Males. I was among the first to head out, but my legs felt like lead before I was even halfway through. Climbing the rope my arms trembled, my palms burning from the coarse fibers. I lost my grip twice before I reached the top. The wall loomed ahead, taller than it had any right to be, and for a split second, I almost stopped. But that same stubborn spark that had kept me alive all these years pushed me forward. I hauled myself over, scraped palms and all, the wood catching at my cammies as I swung a leg over and dropped to the other side. It was not pretty: I fell. But I got up.

Every obstacle in that course felt like a reflection of the life I had lived what I'd faced in life: Rejection, loneliness, feeling less than, yearning to overcome but failing. This time failure had no place. The rope climb was the years I'd spent clawing my way out of situations that should have broken me. The wall was every barrier someone else had put in my way, daring me to prove I could climb higher. The low crawl under barbed wire was the times I'd kept my head down and pushed through pain because there was no other choice. The balance beams were the moments I had to steady myself on nothing but instinct, trusting my own footing when no one was there to guide me.

And just like life, there was no skipping an obstacle. You faced it, or you failed. I came out in 3rd place, good enough for a nobody like me.

Graduation day came, and the stands were packed full of happy families there to congratulate their daughter, sister, mother, or friend. But they were empty for me. I knew not to look for any familiar faces. No one was there for me. Not a single person.

My mother's words had already carved their place in my soul: She could have whispered it instead of spitting it at me through the only phone call I had been allowed in ten weeks, and it still would have landed like a knockout punch.

"Well, I didn't go to your brother's graduation. Why would I even consider going to yours?"

What she really meant was clear to me. In her eyes, I would never measure up to the love she felt for my brother, her favorite child. I was the one who came up short, the one who didn't fit into her narrative. I had grown up in his shadow, always just outside the light. It was not his fault. He also did not choose to be born.

I stood there in my uniform, the sun catching the brim of my cover, the stiff wool collar itching at my neck, and I realized this moment didn't need a single outside witness to be real to me. I knew. I had done this. No one had helped me. My platoon mates and my Drill Instructors supported me, yes, but no one did it for me. I did this.

My Senior Drill Instructor walked with me back to the barracks to retrieve my things, her usual bark softened just slightly, showing respect. Over the weeks she had come to see my family situation, no matter how many letters I sent out, the only letters I had received were from my brother who was also a Marine. I asked her for a way to go straight to my duty station rather than going back to Nebraska for family leave, but that option wasn't available. She told me to go home and be proud of what I had done. The bus came to take me to the airport. I wistfully looked out the window as did several male Marines, wondering if this solitude would be all I ever knew. I wish I had been worldly enough to know I could have rented a hotel for those two weeks, spared myself the weight of returning to a place that had never felt like home and where I was not welcomed when I arrived.

Looking back, I now realize boot camp was a forge. Every mile run in the cold, every shouted correction, every aching muscle was heat and hammer, shaping steel where there had once been uncertainty. Those 12 weeks were not the end of my life battles. But it was the first place I stood my ground and proved, to myself if to no one else, that I deserved to walk in the light, even if I had to light that fire myself.

Still

I didn't want or plan to get pregnant.

It was the first night I met him, the first time we had sex. Freedom, impulsiveness and loneliness make a dangerous cocktail. But I'd spent enough nights staring at the ceiling with no one coming home, and no one special waiting for me at home. No letters from family, just bills and the echo of my own mind. When he offered comfort, I said yes.

Only 4 weeks later, when the test turned out positive, I didn't even cry. One part of me said, well this is another failure. Another part of me was immediately thrilled. This would be my purpose. My second chance. I could create my own little family.

We moved in together because it was the "right" thing to do. It wasn't romance or happily ever after. It was survival. Two scared people, trying to build something with spit and hope and an unplanned pregnancy.

One night, in those exhausted, blurry weeks when a pregnant belly starts to stretch just enough to feel foreign, but looks like a half a volleyball, I was resting on the couch. The weight of fatigue of the day crushing me and the baby crushing my ribs. His friend stopped by. They didn't know I was half awake to hear the conversation.

"She *says* it's mine, but who knows" he said, casually, with the same nonchalant attitude one would reply when a cute waitress when she asks if the cold fries served to you were good.

I never said a word. What could I say? I was just the girl on the couch with a bulging stomach and no ring. I remember staring at the shadows on the ceiling and wondering if my baby heard him.

As the baby grew, it was a tough little one. In my heart I grew to love my son. He kicked early and often, pressing his full foot so hard against my belly so you could see the outline. He was going to be a rough-and-tumble perfect boy. I dreamed of running through fields with a little boy in a crew cut, a white T-shirt with rolled-up sleeves, little Levi's jeans, and bare feet. George was his name. George Strait was my favorite country singer.

The pregnancy wasn't easy. I found out the baby wasn't growing like he should. Another failure. The doctor said we'd induce early. We would make it work out as a team.

The morning of the ultrasound and scheduled induction, I was busy nesting. I took a long, warm bath in my old clawfoot tub, relaxing and talking softly to my son. He seemed to love being in the water, rolling this way and that.

"Tomorrow," I whispered, "you'll be here. And I'll never be alone again."

After the bath and bonding session, I filled the fridge. Stocked the deep freezer. Diapers, fresh fruits, emergency formula, frozen enchiladas, tiny socks, pizzas and baby wipes. Everything he and I should need for at least a week, maybe two. I cleaned. I vacuumed. I imagined what it would feel like to come home with a perfect, tiny, breathing reason to keep going. I was tired, but excited. I thought, thank goodness, I'd be able to rest after the birth. I could be home focusing on my baby.

At the ultrasound, the usually chatty technicians were quiet. Not just serious, but hollow-eyed. They didn't show me things out on the screen like usual. They did not play the heartbeat sound. No pointing out a little hand waving. Just took cold, quiet measurements, whispered medical jargon I had not heard before.

"You have to go to your doctor's office."

I was immediately irritated. I'd done everything the doctor and I had planned. I was ready to be admitted upstairs right after the ultrasound. This was just another unnecessary step, and I was already so tired. I just wanted to go upstairs to the maternity ward and rest. Tonight, or tomorrow, I would hold my son in my arms.

In the doctor's office, the words came like a wrecking ball.

"They say there is no heartbeat. Let me take a listen and see what is going on."

I gasped. Not like in movies. Not a dramatic scream. I just… couldn't breathe.

"But he moved," I said, tears pouring out like blood. "He moved this morning. I was in the bath…"

The doctor tried using a doppler to locate the baby's heartbeat. He could not find a sound.

I curled up in the corner of the office like a feral animal.

He had been my doctor since I was 13. He drove me back to the hospital himself. Redid the ultrasound. His tears fell on my huge protruding useless stomach.

"I am so, so sorry, there is nothing that can be done for the baby. It has passed."

"Get it out," I begged. "Take him out right now. I can donate the organs. Saves someone else's child. Please let his life mean something."

He told me no. Too small. Too far along. Too early. Too late. Too dead.

I begged for a C section, but he recommended a "natural" birth.

"It will be easier for you to recover physically."

He walked me upstairs to the delivery wing sidestepping every nurse that I knew from the hospital tours. He gave them sharp glances and a slight shaking of his head. He was looking for someone in particular. He finally found her. He left me in the hands and care of a nurse who looked like she had overseen every army hospital in World War 2. Tall, no nonsense, a straight shooter.

"Come on in, nothing to cry about right now, be plenty of time for that later." She chirped

"There will be time for tears later. Get changed, shower if you want and get settled in the bed. You are here for the duration of this and so am I."

. Her words came out like the staccato of a machine gun, quickly, leaving no room for pain, but still hurtful, killing the intended issue, all at the same time just provided instructions clear as a bell. She spoke in a way that was harsh and caring at the same time.

True to her word, she was there with me most of the next 3 days and nights. She would walk in, brisk like a cold wind, her old-fashioned nurses' hat firmly fixed to her hair, pin on her sweater looking like she walked out of an episode of *Call The Midwife*.

She would give me some information to digest, then breeze out like giving birth to a dead baby was the most natural thing on earth. She gave me mortuary numbers. Information about autopsy. Explained why there would be no legal Certificate of Birth and that by law my child had never existed since it would not take its first breath. She would take handprints and footprints for a hospital keepsake certificate copy when the time came. She promised to keep the birth as normal as possible, with time to hold the baby and ask any questions. She left the Fetal Death Certificate for me to fill in the needed information. All little digestible matter of fact bites, given every 45 minutes when she came to check my Iv line and more when she brought me my last supper. After midnight tonight, only fluids, and very little of that by mouth she explained.

As much as I wanted to run away from the hospital, keeping my baby inside and not facing the truth, I knew she was right. She doled out the cold hard truth of the matter at hand. Not unfeeling, not rude, just the cold harsh dead truth.

Then the medicine she gave me did the deed.

Labor came. Labor for a child who would never cry, never latch, never need the clothes, bedding, diapers I had so proudly bought. The tiny diapers in my home would end up at a shelter for women, as for the formula and clothing: I would return what I could and donate the rest. All the baby shower gifts I supposed would be returned to the givers.

Two long horrible days of labor later, in the still of the early morning hours, the nurse laid a tiny, swaddled bundle in my arms. I was face to face with my failure. So perfect. So terribly damaged. So still. I unwrapped the bundle trying to memorize every detail. Long, tiny fingers that I imagined would have played the piano. Arms that would never reach out to me. Muscular legs with the feet that I recognized pushing through my abdomen. A mouth that would never nurse, cry, never call for Mama. Open cuts on the scalp that did not even bleed. Tiny bald patches from internal monitors. Bruises and swelling from being head down without blood circulation for 3 days. I took it all in.

No new baby breath, no new baby smell. Instead, the blanket covering the tiny 4-pound body smelled clinical, like starch and hospital air. Even though I was grieving and wanted to die myself, I could not bond with a dead child. It did not feel as if it was what had grown in me for nearly a year.

When I was asked if I wanted a picture. I declined. *I wanted to remember my child alive, or not at all.* Army nurse insisted and I regret now that I did not at least try harder to get some decent pictures. My face was swollen from crying and the punishment of the grueling labor as well as having been pumped full of medications. The baby was purple and blue and swollen as well. Two days of being dead and upside down would do that to someone. Muscles not alive cannot reform the conehead of a long-delayed birth.

They took clinical pictures in the hospital nursery, but they are not able to be displayed. They told me her cord had been horribly malformed. If she had survived, she probably would be severely mentally damaged due to long term lack of oxygen. Those violent kicks, rolls, and tumbles were just her trying to get oxygen. One in a million chances of happening, that somehow happened again to both my subsequent children.

Another life failure. Another loss of a planned future.

I again felt like a failure. I even got the sex wrong: Sammantha was a girl, not the beloved George that I dreamed of and prayed for.

I held her. I whispered apologies. Promises that would never come true. Sweet names I'd never get to call out loud. I said her name. I fell asleep and when I woke, she was gone. There was only a set of handprints and footprints in her place. That is when it truly hit me.

There are no words for that moment. Just a silence that echoes across your soul like a scream that never stops.

3 am

She is not breathing!

It started like any other night with a newborn. It was 3 a.m., and I was in the living room cradling my fussy premature baby girl, exhausted beyond words. If you're a mom, you know those hours: Where your body runs on fumes, the line between day and night disappears, and you can't remember the last time you slept or even ate without interruption.

My life was pretty full this year: I also had a toddler, 18 months old, who clung to her daddy like he hung the moon: They were both asleep blissfully on the other side of the house. I was a full-time student at Central Community College in Hastings, Nebraska, attending classes in person, because back then, online school wasn't an option, and we needed the grant money to keep our little family going. Adding to my stress was an old-fashioned husband who expected dinner on the table, laundry folded, and a perfectly clean home. Life was a tightrope, and I was always seconds from falling apart.

To make matters worse, our newly placed used trailer house had become infested by carpenter ants. We had fought them off ourselves for weeks, sealing everything in bags, scrubbing every inch of the house daily, only to finally give in and call an exterminator. They showed up and told us the chemical "should be okay" for the cat, but not once did they ask about my premature newborn. Looking back now, I think what the hell? How did I not question them? How did I not question myself?

The pregnancy had been one long nightmare. I started labor at 12 weeks. Yes, twelve. From that moment on, I was in and out of the hospital for nearly five months. She was born at 32 weeks, tiny and fragile, but she fought. Oh, she fought so hard. She tried climbing the incubator with her tiny feet during her two-week NICU stay. She rolled over in it more than once. She had to learn to suck, breathe and swallow because she was born too soon. Once she did, she devoured her breast milk, previously given by tube or bottle because she would get exhausted too easily. But she had willpower. This baby had grit. I loved that tiny little girl with everything I had to give.

That night, as I rocked her, I thought she had finally fallen asleep. She had stopped fussing and let out a long exhale. I waited a minute and then did

44

the old mom trick: Lift the arm and let it drop. Thump. Limp. Perfect. Time to put her in the bassinet.

As I stood up, something felt wrong. Her weight shifted oddly against me. I pulled her back into my chest, looked down and panic exploded within me. Her color was off. Her arms were not limp from sleeping; her entire tiny body was limp and bluish purple. Her little face looked…wrong. I instinctively knew: She is not breathing!

Everything inside me screamed, but my mouth would not let the sound come out. My legs moved before my mind did. I ran to the bedroom, screamed at my husband, told him I was taking the baby to the hospital. He rolled over, mumbled, "Okay," and went back to sleep. I stared at him for a second, frozen between disbelief and fury. Fine. He could stay with our other daughter, who adored him anyway. They had spent so much time together during my hospital trips.

Hopefully this time he remembered he had a child. And I'll never forget when our firstborn was just three months old, he left her home alone for over an hour. I had driven his brother to the bus stop 25 miles away. He said he forgot. How do you forget that you have a newborn child?

But right then, I didn't have time to think about that or be angry. I started CPR, breathless with fear, whispering and screaming her name over and over, willing her to come back to me. And then finally, she shuddered. Her chest rose. She sucked in a sharp breath and went still again. Relief rushed through me like a tidal wave. She was just sleeping, I thought. Just tired.

But no. She was still completely limp. She was not breathing. My daughter had died in my arms. I did another round of CPR, and she came around. I had brought her back to life, but would she remain alive this time? I grabbed a blanket to cover her from the freezing night air and snow, grabbed her portable car seat and some cash. I placed her in the passenger seat of my old car, praying it would start. I drove, sliding on the ice of last night's snowstorm. I kept one hand on the wheel, the other lightly shaking her to keep her crying. A crying baby is a living baby.

I got to the hospital, parked in the ER zone and ran into the cold Nebraska night, holding her to my chest like my own heartbeat could keep her alive. At that moment, I wasn't a college student. I wasn't a wife. I was just a terrified mother praying for her baby to live.

I ran into the hospital screaming like a mad woman that my child was not breathing. The intake nurse tried to reason with me, that the baby was crying so she was breathing. I was not having it. An orderly came and took the baby as I followed behind. She was still blue, despite crying laboriously. Her oxygen was low and after they stabilized her, she was admitted.

Tests later showed that she was allergic to a chemical used in the fumigation of the house. Even though I had taken precautions and stayed somewhere else overnight and aired it out, it would not have mattered. She spent a week in hospital then came home on a heart monitor.

That night never left me.

She survived it. So did I. Something took hold in me and at the same time broke that night. Or maybe something was born. Some part of me knew I was on my own in this life, with my two daughters. That the cavalry wasn't ever coming. There was no Superman. That I had to be the one to keep fighting, to keep breathing. For her, for her sister, and for me.

Provision in a Pawn Shop

Never once did I lose my faith in God, even though I often questioned it.

I came close. There were many times in my life when I felt abandoned by people I loved, by churches I trusted, even by the communities I tried so hard to serve.

Even when I had every reason to throw in the towel, I had not. Every time I failed, every time I fell short or felt completely empty, I was still alive. Still held. Still carried. Still provided for.

God always found a way to reach me.

One year, when we were living in Nebraska, my oldest daughter had just started high school and had worked extremely hard all season in cross-country. As a freshman, she earned her varsity athletic letter. That doesn't come easy and was not common for a freshman especially when she was the youngest person on the team. It meant the world to her.

In most schools, when a student earns that varsity letter, parents can buy what's called a letterman's jacket. It is warm, heavy coat with the school's colors, the student's name, and the letter sewn proudly onto the chest. It's a rite of passage. A symbol of grit and effort. She wanted that jacket badly, and I wanted to give it to her.

I had about $500 saved. My plan was to use $300 for the jacket and then surprise her with something even more special. While she was away for the weekend, I would redecorate her bedroom. Something meaningful, all in the spirit of her passions: tigers for her team and running. She loved both. It was going to be a "While You Were Out" moment: A complete transformation while she was gone. Paint, new bedding, small decorations all done by her sister and I with love and a little creativity.

But then, the youth group at the local church in Hastings announced a weekend retreat for the teens. The cost was $100 per child. I signed my daughter up immediately. This was a good thing, and I hoped it would speak to her in ways a new jacket couldn't. Then I felt a nudge to ask the pastor if there's a child who needs help. So, I did. He gave me a name. Then my daughter came to me, eyes shining, and asked if we could help another friend go too. Without hesitation, I said yes.

Just like that, $300 of the $500 was gone, driving down the road in a church van with 3 happy youth in the back seat waving goodbye. And the jacket? The room makeover? They seemed out of reach now. I had no idea how I could make my dream "While You Were Out" vision come true.

With only $200 left, my younger daughter and I set out on a small but disheartening adventure. We didn't have a real plan, just a bit of hope and a whisper of faith. We went to thrift stores and discount shops. We were looking for anywhere I thought I could stretch a dollar further than it wanted to go. Then we walked across the street to another discount store beside a pawn shop.

There in the window, as if it had been waiting for us, was a letterman's jacket. The exact jacket we needed.

Her school colors. Her size. Her style. $100. It looked brand new.

I stood there for a moment, blinking back tears. Only God could have placed it there.

We bought it. And that left us with $100.

Exactly what I had already spent for some paint, blankets, and tiger-themed decorations for her room. We had printed some pictures at the library and got a few frames from a thrift store. My younger daughter helped me pick out each item with joy and I encouraged her to use her crafty talents to make something work. I told her I was happy we got the weekend together, that I hoped we would all 3 remember it forever. We ate popcorn and drank Pepsi and watched movies as we stayed awake late through the night hand sewing the H letter onto the jacket.

We spent the weekend painting, rearranging, and creating a space that said to her sister:

"We see you and your accomplishments. We celebrate you and what you have achieved. We are so proud of you, you can do anything you put your mind to. You are so loved."

When my daughter came home and walked into her new room, her sister was there holding her brand-new letterman's jacket, she gasped. Then she cried. I cried too.

I had learned what it was like to grow up unseen and unwanted. I never wanted my children to know those feelings. I am sure I failed many times. But I did want them to have the best. I just did not know how.

I didn't know how to make the money work, either. But God did—every single time.

Pearls in the Rubble

I've lived through all kinds of disasters: Emotional, relational, physical, health, and financial.

But the natural disasters? Those are the ones that always seem to wash something clean in me—stripping me down to the barest essentials yet somehow leaving me more whole than before.

Back in 2005, I was living in Nebraska during the year of Hurricane Katrina and Wilma. But while the wind was tearing through the Gulf Coast as Katrina barreled down on it, a different kind of storm was unfolding in my own life. She was the largest physical storm ever, but even Katrina was not as big as the emotional storm I was fighting in myself.

I had just made the hardest decision I'd ever made. I left my husband.

I walked out of our brand-new home taking my two daughters, not a whole lot of money, a heart aching from years of pain, and a body that could finally start healing after years of physical abuse. I didn't know what would come next. Just that we couldn't stay in the old life.

That Sunday, I walked into a new church, anxious, nervous and worn thin. Of all the biblical books they could've started teaching on, it was Nehemiah. A story about a man rebuilding the walls of a broken city.

Rebuilding a city... or a life.

Each chapter felt like it was written just for me. Nehemiah started by securing the gates. He took stock of the damage. He assigned people to the tasks they could handle. He made sure the widows and children were protected. He reminded them that even a city (or life) in total ruins could be salvaged and even sanctified and holy, if only you kept your eyes on God.

It all sank deep into my heart. I had nothing and I was rebuilding. It lit a fire in my daughters also.

That Christmas, we decided not to buy each other gifts. Instead, we planned a trip to bring joy to kids who had lost everything to hurricane Katrina. We'd lost a lot too, but others had lost even more. Somehow, giving felt like healing. When we told people what we were doing, blessings just started pouring in. Someone donated a truck bed cover for my pickup to keep the gifts dry and secure. Others offered us safe places to stay on the road. Right before we left, a family who was upgrading their home computers donated the old ones for kids who didn't have any. One after another, doors opened. Gifts appeared.

By the time we packed the truck, it was full: Topper to tailgate with toys, clothes, essentials, and hope.

I called a Head Start program in New Orleans, but by some twist, I got redirected to a small Head Start in another county. One that had been hit just as hard, but that had been completely overlooked. No help had come their way. Not yet.

We told them we were coming.

They were kind and grateful but concerned. The neighborhood was rough, they warned us. The housing project we would have to go into had been plagued with looting and violence. It would be better if we just left the gifts at the center.

"You shouldn't go in there," they said. "You could be robbed. Or worse."

I told my daughters: "God didn't bring us this far to leave us now." I had already decided.

In we went. And what happened next still feels like a dream.

We were met not with fear, anger or violence. We were met with open arms. The children's eyes lit up with joy as we handed out gifts. Some were used, some new, but all chosen with love. My girls gave out blankets, books, crayons, and little toys. They smiled, knelt down to hug little ones, and laughed with kids who'd nearly lost everything that year. We made sure they could still enjoy the Magic of Christmas. The younger daughter told me we must have been like the 3 Wise Men: bringing presents to someone we had never met, knowing that maybe the world could be changed because of it.

As I watched the faces of my daughters, glowing with generosity, compassion, and something sacred: Giving. I couldn't tell which was more beautiful: The faces of the children receiving, or the faces of my children giving. They were 12 and 14 years old and they gave away their entire Christmas season for this moment. At the age where fashion was important, they got no new clothes, makeup, or shoes. They gave all. I will always admit that my daughters are better people than I am.

We ended up staying with a cousin near the Mississippi Coast for a few days before we took the long trek back North. We attended a Christmas celebration of nearly 60 family members, ones from my father's side, most of whom we had never met. Most of whom had lost everything to Katrina, but they still had their family.

My dear sweet Aunt Jo came and asked me to go to her bedroom for a talk. Good ole imposter syndrome came with us: I was sure she was going to tell me not to come back. Instead that beautiful woman wrapped me up in the biggest bear hug and with tears in her eyes she explained to me a different life story than what I knew. She told me she blamed my father for never going to get me. She explained that when I was about 3 years old, my grandmother had gone to visit, to see if I was being raised properly and had come back telling my father he needed to get me away from my mother. She told me of nights she prayed, feeling that something was not right, and how she begged my father to go get me and my sister. She had offered to raise us along with the own children and stepchildren. Two more would not have made a difference, she had explained to him. Why he never came for us, he never told me.

I will forever think of my Aunt Jo as my Mama Jo. She is the only person outright named in this memoir. She changed my life that day and gave me hope for the future. She gave me the foundation to consider that I was actually worthy.

We had all promised not to exchange presents. We had given our Christmas to God. That was the gift. But as if God couldn't help Himself, my cousin surprised us with something small and meaningful.

Three oyster shells.

Each one looked rough and battered, like it had been through the same emotional storm we had. The same physical storm the coast had been through. We sat there struggling to open them, giggling as we tried to crack them just right. And inside each weathered shell?

A pearl. A soft, shining, perfect pearl.

And isn't that just like life?

Sometimes the ugliest shells hold the most beautiful treasures. Sometimes, the worst storms lead us to the best chapters. And sometimes, when you give everything to God, He gives you back something even better.

Not because you asked for it.

But because He delights in showing you that there's beauty still to be found like a beautiful pearl right there in the rubble.

Running to Her Own Dream

My eldest daughter was once the talk of her high school: The first girl in over twenty years from our town to qualify for the state cross country meet.

Now, if you've never been to a state cross-country meet, let me paint the picture: Hundreds of the fastest, most determined teenagers in the state, all gathering to race over hills, through mud, against wind, and across open fields. It's not just running. It's grit in motion. It's lungs burning and legs trembling but never quitting.

It's a sport where pain is part of the process, heart is as important as training, and finishing strong is everything.

My beautiful daughter had more natural running talent in her baby finger than most adults muster in their lifetime. It had shown up in middle school. Without any training or special gear, she signed up and finished yards before the other girls, and her times beat almost every boy in both the 800m run and 1600m run. The high school coaches were there, and they asked her if she was interested in running both cross country and track. That was the beginning of her running career.

That Fall, Cross Country came first. She stepped into her new passion like a Princess: She annihilated other girls. She trained with the boys because the girls couldn't keep up.

There were 2 and 3 school meets. She danced over the finish line with no one behind her for 10-20 meters. As the season went on, at the conference championship meet she dominated again. Districts came and people started to watch her, cheer for her, and she broke a record, landing the chance to go to the State meet at the same time. The team did not make it, but she did in individual time.

One boy from her school, the one she trained with most often, also made it to state. As a freshman competing against all the 9-12 grades in the state, she came in 10th. Her first experience with something this big and she acted as it were nothing. The next year she went back and got fifth, still competing against students much older than her.

Springtime came and she did it again during high school track season She still trained with the boys. She would run several long races in one day at the meets: 800m individual, 1600m individual, 3200 individual 3200 m relay often all in one day!

Again, she was the fastest and best runner the school had seen in decades.

I knew my girl was different. Special. Blessed. Everything I wasn't. She was light where I had known only weight. She was fast and free when my life had been stuck in survival mode. She was popular, she was beautiful, she excelled in both sports and school.

Then the colleges started calling. There were six offers to run at their schools, maybe more. I thought I've finally done something right. It was too late for me, but for her, she was getting the breaks I did not.

I tried to give her everything I never had to help her career. The right coach? We changed schools. Proper gear? I made sure she had every pair of shoes she needed. A private trainer? Of course. I didn't care what it took. I wanted her to have all the advantages I'd dreamed of but never got. I didn't want to be her. I just wanted her to have the opportunity to be the absolute best she could be with the talent she had. To thrive. To never feel like she wasn't enough. I bought the right food, the right drinks, I was there at every meet if her or a teammate needed something.

On National Athlete Signing Day, we drove 4 hours up to Dana College. They rolled out the red carpet for us. She was the star of the show, and I got to sit beside her front row. Her stepfather even came with us to show how proud he was. The pictures they took that day? They looked like something out of the NFL draft. There she was, wearing her Dana t-shirt, glowing, signing papers with a smile that still warms me to this day. That photo is still taped to my refrigerator. Not just for her, though she earned it, but also for me. A reminder. Proof that I had poured my heart into this daughter who turned out amazing.

At the end of her first college year, she was crowned best student athlete in the entire school.

She had done it. We had done it. And at that moment, I was more than just her mother. Maybe I was the person who supplied bones and rafters for her, but she was the architect of her own dream.

An Unsaid Goodbye

No one knew the truth.
They thought they did.

For months in Nebraska, I planned my next voyage. Both loudly, out in the open, and quietly, with a hidden plan. I sold almost everything I owned, clothes, furniture, books. Literally everything I said I couldn't carry. I gave what I could to charity, telling people it was for a big move. Moving from Nebraska to Mississippi, I said. A fresh start a year after my divorce. A new life.

No one guessed the truth: I was planning to end it all.

I wanted to disappear. To stop the pain inside that no one really saw. I was tired—bone-deep tired. I had fought this pain for years. I had failed once again. I was divorced. I had wanted to stay married, but I could not continue to live in or raise my daughters in the abusive environment we were in. I did not want to die; I just wanted the pain of being a failure to end. My truths had gotten to me again. I saw no hope.

But when the moment came, it didn't go as I thought it would. I had a plan so carefully mapped out—but God and the Universe had other ideas.

Against my best-laid plans, my attempt to end my life failed. I was left broken, mangled in an automotive wreck that took more than just my body. It took away the faith others had in me. It took my ability to care for myself for quite a while. My back was broken in seven places. Learning to move again felt like climbing a mountain every single day. Learning to walk freely again was a reminder of what I lost. And what my family lost too.

My children didn't just lose an able-bodied parent. They lost the version of me they could believe in. I could not hug them without shaking. I could not laugh with them without crying in pain. I could not be their safe place. My emotional absence carved deep wounds that may never heal. Once again, I was a failure. This time, I let down more than just myself.

My youngest daughter became my caretaker. She set up my pills and snacks for the day before leaving for school. She was a senior in high school. At night, she would help me shower. There are few things more humbling in your 40's than having your teenage daughter wash you and help you change your soiled diaper. The silence around why it had happened made it harder for all of us. Eventually, she began taking me out to walk at stores because Walmart and Walgreens had smooth floors and wide, easy-to-navigate aisles where I had room for a wheelchair, then walker.

I recovered the first eight weeks on a couch in a cousin's home. She had a friend who came by every week to visit, always bringing McDonald's for anyone who might be there. He always offered me a hamburger, and the first time I accepted, he celebrated like it was a birthday. Food had not been a priority, my appetite and ability to eat had been dulled by medication and pain. The first time I got off the couch without help and stood at the bar counter, everyone in the house celebrated again. It sounded like a touchdown at the Super Bowl. For Christmas, they took me to a party at the American Legion in a wheelchair so I could be part of the celebration without tiring too quickly.

Recovery wasn't just physical. It was a struggle to rebuild trust and hope in my life and in my own self. I saw my daughter happy that I was alive, but we were both scared of what we were going through. Some days, I thought about giving up again. But somehow, I found reasons to keep putting one foot in front of the other.

I learned that surviving isn't just about me. It's about the people who love you and believe in you even when you feel like you're alone, those who offer help and understanding.

Sometimes, the hardest thing was to let them. To allow people into my life, to let them see the broken parts, and for me to see that they still believe I was worth loving and fighting for.

Walking into a New Life

"What are your goals?"

The question seemed simple enough, but it hit harder than I expected. I looked up at the physical therapist, making no effort to hide the exhaustion behind my eyes.

"To walk and text at the same time," I said. "And to climb the Biloxi Lighthouse."

He laughed. A full bellied laugh: Not in a mocking way, but the kind of genuine laugh that says, now that's something real.

"Probably the most legitimate goals I've heard all week," he said.

But nothing about how I got there was funny.

I was recovering from a broken back: Seven shattered vertebrae. I had been a passenger in a car driven by someone I had cared for very much. Someone who'd whispered promises and pain until we both believed dying together made more sense than living apart. It was a suicide pact: one I hadn't fully agreed to, not able to speak it out loud, but silently enough that it still haunts me. I did not want to die; I just wanted my internal pain to end.

The car crashed in a horrific way, as we planned.

I woke up alone in the hospital, and he never came back. Not to the hospital, not to my life. In 2024, my friend succeeded. I hope God gave him the freedom he sought.

The doctors saved me. They pieced me back together with rods, screws, and the kind of skill that leaves you grateful and grieving at the same time. Then came the brutal, unforgiving complications: A twisted bowel, internal bleeding. Fourteen units of blood were transfused, and still no one could tell me where the blood was going or why I was dying so slowly. Yet somehow, eventually, I lived. Again, I had failed. I felt I was so screwed up that I had even failed at killing myself.

I was weak. Broken. I couldn't sit up, couldn't roll over, or stand without help. They brought me a walker, a brace that wrapped around my torso like a prison, and pitying eyes that followed me everywhere.

But I didn't want pity. I wanted strength. I wanted control. I wanted to walk down the hall and carry my own damn Jello cup. I wanted to text while I walked, like any other person just trying to live their life. We began the work. Day after day, I shuffled, I cried, I fell. My physical therapist became my coach, my witness, my confessor. With every step, I felt every screw in my back. With every gain, it seemed like 3 steps back.

Five months after the surgery, I stood in my bathroom, staring at myself in the mirror. My body was marked by trauma—muscles atrophied, scars still healing—but I had made it this far. I took off the back brace slowly, like shedding a second skin. It felt dangerous. It felt like freedom. I put it back on, not knowing how many more months I would be trapped inside it.

That day, I went to the swimming pool. Again, I took off my cage, and I walked into the water. Heart pounding, I dove in. It wasn't graceful, nothing about recovery is. But it was my day, my time of freedom, if only for a few short minutes. The cold wrapped around me like a second chance. I swam and cried and floated on my back, looking at the sky, feeling as though I had finally broken the surface after drowning far too long.

I wasn't just surviving anymore. I was free. I was strong. I was a woman who would one day climb the Biloxi Lighthouse.

And I did. One month later, I received the doctor's order that allowed me to be completely free: My back had fuses enough that I could remove the brace except in any instance of dangerous activity, which was prohibited for life. No horseback riding, bungie jumping, or carnival rides for the rest of my life.

I held the railing and climbed slowly, carefully. With every step, I whispered thank you. To my body, to my soul, to God, and to the part of me that never gave up. I even thanked the part of me that had failed. I reached the top of that beautiful pure white lighthouse that had stood as a promise and a challenge every time I passed it going to therapy. The wind kissing my face, the sea stretching out before me.

I stood tall. I texted my family. And I smiled.

Because I had walked. And I had texted. And I had climbed.

All at the same time.

Bones, Sweat, and Clawfoot Dreams

Shortly after leaving Nebraska and moving to Mississippi, my youngest daughter and I began shopping for a new home. Not a brick or wood building or house: A Home. A place that we could create our new lives, and that would brim with life, love and happiness.

We must have walked through thirty houses in half as many days, and every one of them felt wrong: Too shiny, too far away from town, too fancy of a neighborhood, or just not our style. We were about ready to stop looking. My daughter finally challenged the realtor:

"Look, we are paying cash, we have it in hand, and you still cannot find us something that we can fix up? You get two more houses. After that we will just search on our own."

Then we saw The University House.

From the outside, it didn't look like much. The brick was old and needed tuckpointed. The tired chain-link fence waws sagging in many places. The corner lot that had seen better days and now had given up trying. But when we stepped inside, the air and the attitude shifted. My daughter's boots crunched over broken tile, her eyes wide like she'd stumbled onto a gold vein. She didn't see rot and dust; she saw possibility.

"These bones are strong," she said, running her hand along the exposed frame of a half-demolished wall. "We can work with this. Mama: What if we pull down this wall?"

Without that one wall, the house was wheelchair and walker friendly, and we both knew that someday I may end up back in an assistive device someday. My back and my leg were healing, but the doctor could not predict my long-term future. For sure, there would be no marathons for me in the future.

This tiny 90-pound soaking wet teenager knew more about construction than most grown men and could outwork most of them also. She liked the house immediately. I did too. It had "bones" and was safe enough to live in while we remodeled it. I paid $27,000 cash for that HUD repossession. It was in worst neighborhood in the county, but it was on a main street, right across from a school, and a corner lot.

It had promise. It was no one's dream house, but in a record time of 2 weeks, it was ours.

I had my daughter come to every meeting, every document signing that it took to finish the purchase. She was even the one who handed over the check. I wanted her to teach her how the process worked. I wanted to give her a gift of carrying that knowledge into her own future, just like I'd done with each of my children's first cars. No one had taught me anything growing up about these things: I wanted them to at least have some basics of finance.

Us two Nebraska girls set out to set their roots in Mississippi clay, and this beat-up house became our shared project, our new chapter. It was abused enough to be affordable, but strong enough to carry the weight of our rebuild.

The surprises started fast. On our second day, a police officer pulled up slow, parked, and leaned against his cruiser, and said politely, "Ma'am, I'd recommend you bring in your tools each night and get security cameras up as soon as you can. Welcome to the neighborhood, I guess."

We just stared at him and each other in disbelief. Cameras? Well, we weren't in Nebraska anymore.

Neighbors wandered over, eyeing our stacks of lumber, sheetrock and buckets of nails that we were currently moving into the house instead of leaving in the front driveway. We would use one bedroom to store all of it. Surprise! Now we have to work around the supplies.

"Y'all fixing it up for a HUD rental? Let me know when ya ready. I wanna get my fam to stay there when it's done." At least 8 people all asked the same question in various forms.

"Nope," we'd answer without missing a beat. "We're going to live here. This is our home."

The reaction was almost always the same—wide-eyed, baffled:

"But… you're white."

We'd just laugh. "Oh, you noticed that too?"

Everyone would have a good laugh at the two white Northerners coming to live in "The Hood." It was difficult to convince them that Nebraska was actually South of the Mason-Dixon Line.

We eventually learned that the neighborhood was 99 percent black. We were the 1% white. It was known for selling drugs and the school across the two-lane street had the lowest test scores and attendance rates in the county. After we put in the security cameras, we saw many drug deals and police stops outside our front door. After a while, the neighborhood teens started calling me "White Madea" for my no-nonsense way of dealing with things. It was all new to us, and we took to it like snow white ducks out of water.

Doing hard work and construction weren't new to us. My ex-husband had been a contractor and a perfectionist, which meant redoing plenty of work to his standards. This time, the standards were our own. We were building for ourselves, not for approval. That year, I watched my daughter transform into a true construction worker, an adult, a leader, but most of all a Lady Boss who could swing a hammer and hold her ground.

We both knew respect wasn't given, it was earned.

Both for us and the people we hired, we worked hard every day. Contractors were expected to do the same. We hired the occasional passerby who said they wanted to work, laying down the rules plain: show up at 8 a.m. sharp. Not 8:01, not 8:05. By noon, we'd sit on paint buckets around a scrap of plywood, sharing pizza or sandwiches. If they lasted the morning, we'd ask if they wanted to stay for the afternoon shift. Most didn't.

Tools went missing at first, until I put my daughter in charge. Not a single tool disappeared after that. I never asked how.

My favorite moment came the day a contractor sliced straight through five original kitchen studs with a circular saw. My daughter didn't blink. "Those studs are coming out of your pay," she told him. "They're old, strong, dry and original. You'll buy replacements." She deducted the cost herself when she cut his check.

Most of the work, though, was done by the two of us alone. Two women, one truck, and more trips to Lowe's than I could count. My brother and nephew flew in from California to help lay tile and hang cabinets. Sometimes we would all linger at Lowe's just to enjoy some air conditioning. It was a welcome break from the Mississippi heat pressing on our backs like a wet towel. We would talk about how different the world was in the South. How things were slower, friendlier, and sweeter: Especially the tea! The first time I drank Southern Sweet Tea I thought I had gotten the glass with all the sugar for the entire pitcher! In those days I watched her mature, starting to become a woman with choices ahead of her and a backbone that would someday support the weight of her own world, instead of being a part of mine.

She kept a running total of our savings through store sales. She encouraged me to use my veteran discount and made sure I showed my card every time. She had one thing in mind: the fiberglass clawfoot tub in the bathroom displays. It was outfitted with a telephone style shower head in gleaming silver plate. Every time I lost track of her in the store, I'd find her lounging in it like she was already home. The workers always let her, they knew there was an AC vent just overhead and she was careful not to scratch it.

Months later, after endless sheetrock chalk and sawdust covered afternoons, the Lowe's employees knew us by name. They started helping us find better deals, smarter solutions. When the store resets its displays, they offered us that clawfoot tub at a huge discount: 50% off. It did have a small scratch on it, but after so much work, so did we.

She got her tub. She got her dream bathroom, right down to the light fixtures.

That summer and the following winter we added small touches. We changed the garage into a teen room, worked on the fence and started a raised garden outside. Fall came and the rebuild was complete. Instead of working all day, we spent time making bonfires outside and lounging on the couch inside with our two new rescue dogs. One was a

Boxer she named Ladydog that we got for "protection." She would probably help a thief carry a tv out she was so sweet! The mini–Jack Russel/Chihuahua mix was Mightydog, for the resemblance the tiny 8-week-old pup had to the package of dog food by the same name.

We didn't just rebuild a house that year. We rebuilt a life. Piece by piece, board by board, we turned that forgotten brick box into a place of belonging. The walls held our laughter and our arguments, our blisters and our pride.

We also helped rebuild part of the community. We arranged to have the concrete gates that announced the neighborhood rebuilt with the Black Christian Men's League. We provided the materials; They did the labor. We contacted the City to have the "University Estates" letters replaced. Then we invited the Boys and Girls club over to plant flowers and have popsicles. We were rebuilding pride in the community with our neighbors.

They no longer climbed on the rubble of a broken wall. Instead, they knocked on the door after school and asked if they could pick some of their own flowers for their mamas and mawmaws. Those moms, grandmothers, and even dads started to wave, stopped by with some extra fruit for sale, and

78

even helped change my child's tire and took the flat to fix it for her once.

The sweetest part about moving to the South was not the house, or even the tea. We learned you don't have to be from somewhere to belong there. You just have to show up. On time, every day. For work, for the neighborhood, but most of all for each other.

Two

Suitcases and a Whole New World

I arrived in Mexico with just two suitcases and a backpack.

That was all I allowed myself. Two old leather suitcases stuffed with what I thought would cover the basics of starting over. Clothes I could mix and match, a couple pairs of sandals, my favorite coffee mug from the Marine Corps wrapped in a sweater, and a few keepsakes I couldn't bear to leave behind. The zippers strained a little, and the handles bore the weight like overworked mules. I told myself I was traveling light, but there's a difference between packing light and packing for a whole new life. Or maybe not any life.

The real "oh shit" moment didn't hit me at the airport. Even though it had been building for days—maybe weeks—it landed fully hours later after my flight landed. The humid air had glued my shirt to my back, and I was standing in front of the Airbnb I'd booked.

The heat was filled with humidity, a damp blanket that made every breath taste faintly of salt and dreams. The main street of the island was

81

nearby and loud, scooters zipping past, horns blaring, and Taxis headed toward the other end of the island, but not back toward town at this hour. Somewhere in the complex the scent of grilled meat. Rich, smoky, edged with garlic was drifting toward the main gate, making my empty stomach twist. I shifted my suitcases from one sore hand to the other and waited for the host to show. No one came. I finally just stacked them up in the only shade I could find: A sliver cast by a leaning palm tree and took a seat. Later as I followed the shade as the sun took its daily journey, I sat on a pile of rubble: The concrete was warm through my jeans, rough against my palms as I braced myself: I began to wonder if once again in my life I had been scammed.

Five minutes passed. Then fifteen. Then an hour. My heart began to pound with that heavy, hollow thud you get when you know the problem isn't going to solve itself. I didn't know enough Spanish to explain my situation if I found someone to ask. I didn't have a backup plan. And more than anything, I didn't know a single person in this city. I was alone in a way I had never been alone before. And I did not speak the language.

I thought back to last night in Lincoln, Nebraska. That was where I spent my last night in the United States of America.

I had checked into a hotel near the airport, the kind with patterned carpet that looks like it's been vacuumed in straight lines for decades. The hallway smelled faintly of industrial cleaner and microwaved popcorn. My brother and his wife met me there for supper. We went to Applebee's, a perfectly ordinary chain restaurant that suddenly felt like a piece of home I might never get back. We ordered the kind of comfort food that has no surprises: The 2 for $25 meals of steak and mashed potatoes and crisp steamed broccoli. A comfort meal for me: It was the same meal no matter what US state it was ordered in. The waitress called us "hon" in that Midwestern way, refilling our iced teas without asking. Mine, sweet, from my time in the South, his plain, the Midwesterner in him. We talked about family, about little nothings, filling the air so it didn't get heavy. Underneath it all, I knew—we both knew—this might be the last time we sat across from each other for years. Maybe longer.

We didn't say goodbye like it was final, but I still tucked every detail away just in case. The way the air smelled faintly of cornfields and snow. The way my brother kept glancing at me like he wanted to say more. I kept my bearing and never gave in to tell him I was afraid. I was not afraid of the move: I was afraid to fail. Again.

The soft scrape of forks against plates, the neon beer signs glowing in the windows. I didn't know when I would sit in an Applebee's again.

"Do they even have Applebee's in Mexico? Pizza Hut? Steakhouse buffets?"

I did not know. I thought that I would return to the USA to visit in the future, but the world seemed out of control in the last few years, and the future was never promised. That thought rode with me through the flight the next morning, tucked somewhere between the fear and my excitement for my new life.

Before this leap, I'd been to Mexico plenty of times. Cozumel had been a regular stop on the cruises I had enjoyed over the last 2 years. I'd stood on the deck at least ten times, watching the island glimmer in the fading sunset as we left, each visit too short to do more than tease what life might be like there. Those trips were like little love affairs— intense, fleeting, and always ending too soon. I'd disembark for the day, wander through the streets in the warm breeze, then sail away again, leaving a piece of myself behind each time. The sea would turn from turquoise and teal and it, as well my feelings, would also turn to a deep endless blue as I left.

This time, I wasn't sailing away. This time, I was here to stay.

Only two weeks before my 50th birthday I was stepping into a whole new country as a single white female. It would have been very different if I'd done it in my twenties. I wasn't here to chase youth or to "find myself" in the romanticized way travel blogs and rom-com movies like to package it. I was here to rewrite the story I'd been trapped in for years. I was going to choose independence over comfort, to risk change instead of clinging to a routine that had grown stale, I was going to try and succeed finally. It was about finally being the boss of my own life, even if that meant fumbling through the basics, mispronouncing words, and learning humility one awkward interaction at a time.

The complete break from family and friends through sheer distance would help them become less dependent on me. I felt that if I was ever really going to be able to end myself, this was a way to do it. Little steps. Make distance so they would not grieve as much when the end came.

That first night, after finally giving up on the Airbnb and finding a small hotel nearby, one that smelled of stale tacos and spilled beer, I sat out on a narrow balcony with a rickety iron railing. I watched two cruise ships sail away in the distance and another level of "Oh Shit" hit me. The street below was alive in a way that seeped into my bones. Vendors called out their prices in rhythmic chants, the scent of roasted corn and chili drifted up to me, and somewhere in the not so distance a mariachi trumpet cut through the warm air. Stray dogs barked from shadowed alleys, scooters whined past, and the laughter from a corner taco stand spilled into the night. I was my first realization that it wasn't background sound. Noise was the heartbeat of this island.

I realized, sitting there with my two suitcases on the bed, that this wasn't just a stop on the map.

It could be my home if I was willing to do the work. If I was willing to learn the language, the customs, the unspoken rules. If I could let the city's rhythm sink into my own. It would be easy to learn to fit in. The perfect cover for a future plan to check out. Or just maybe it would give me a reason to live.

The loneliness that night was sharp, like standing on a pier with the wind cutting through your jacket. It pressed in close, reminding me how far I was from anyone who knew me. But there was also something else beneath it. An undercurrent of excitement, like the hum of a motor just starting up. Every small success in the days ahead was a win. Ordering a meal without pointing at the menu, recognizing a word on a street sign, getting a genuine smile of recognition from a local, all built my confidence in myself.

It would either be a brick laid in the foundation of a new life I was daring to build, or a way to find a way to check out of the world on my own terms. But either way it would come one halting conversation at a time.

The Happiest Day at the Happiest Place on Earth

I have been to Disneyworld exactly three times.

The Happiest Place on Earth? Not for me! I never thought that I would find happiness there. Crowds, crying children everywhere, parents angry at one another over because they missed out on a ride, long lines over an hour, prices beyond the budget of most families, and people pretending to be happy when they were not. Nope, not happy for me!

On my first visit, I was with my daughter, her husband and their baby daughter. My eldest granddaughter had always been a solemn, serious little girl. She laughed at Disneyworld for the very first time. It was with the Belle character from Beauty and the Beast. We were all a little crazy watching her laugh as we encouraged her to do it over and over, like we'd seen magic unfold right in front of us. On the second visit two years later, the magic for us came in an even bigger way.

That same week, after my family left, I went again with my favorite uncle, his amazing wife and my dear beautiful, sweet cousin. I had a great calm relaxing day, because no one wanted to ride the scary rides, we were all adults and the day was about catching up and visiting, not the park. Since they lived nearby, we ate at all the "best" places and had the "best snacks" including a Dole Whip. They knew what time to go where and how to avoid the crowds, too. I enjoyed being in their presence even more, as my uncle had been a safe place for me when I was young.

When we went again, I knew from the beginning it would be an adventure: I gave my daughter a credit card and told her:

"Do it how you dream it."

She did it up right: A whole week, staying on property this time, at Disney's Art of Animation Resort, in the Finding Nemo section. The whole area felt like stepping into the movie—bright blues and corals everywhere, giant statues of Nemo and his friends scattered along the walkways. Our room even had Nemo-themed furniture: the bedspreads patterned with clownfish, the chairs shaped like seashells, and little underwater touches that made us feel like we were sleeping inside the reef. She set up all-inclusive meals, so the children (or me) never had to be told no to a meal, drink or snack.

One afternoon, all of us, my two granddaughters, my daughter, my son-in-law, and "MeMe" (me) spent an hour at the Nemo splash pad. The girls ran through the sprays of water, squealing as giant jellyfish sculptures rained down soft streams, and we all laughed until our cheeks hurt. My daughter and I sat together on the edge, watching tiny bare feet slap across the wet pavement, knowing this was the kind of joy worth traveling for. There was no way to put a price on days like this.

Today, we were at the main park. My sweet, amazing girl was hot, tired, and beyond stressed trying to keep to her dream. I saw her juggling fast passes and character schedules, breastfeeding the littlest one, hydrating the older one, making sure everyone got to see their favorite princess, ride their favorite ride and visit their favorite park and show. She even had a plan to find the Fairy Godmother for me: the plan fell through, but the Godmother found ME by mistake. My daughter just wanted the trip to be perfect. I had no idea how much pressure I'd accidentally put on her until I saw it reflected on her face. I had placed the world on her shoulders when I really only wanted her to be happy.

The understanding of what I had done broke my heart.

I decided I was going to try and fix it. I called Disney customer service and said, very plainly,

"I am not happy at the happiest place on earth."

There was a pause, then the rep said, "Well, let's fix that. How happy would you like to be?"

I replied that I was not able to be in the Shaquille O'Neil or Queen Elizabeth budget-range-happy, but to give me a few ideas and let's see how happy my budget can get me.

We laughed, and then we got serious. The operator told me about different levels of VIP experiences: Unlimited skip the line passes that have a Disney host (I think they called them guest experience guides), and the family could glide from ride to ride like royalty or rock stars. We could choose all day, half day, private or shared with another small group. All the roller coasters, one after the other, or all the classic rides. I found one in my price range and booked it. It was more than I wanted to spend, but fortunately both children were free since they were 3 and under. I splurged on 3 adult VIP passes. Why not? All-inclusive, guided, on-park magic that could lift the burden from my daughter. It was a gift to my daughter, to apologize deeply for every time in her life when I had inadvertently added weight when I meant to lift her.

The morning of our VIP Day started with one of Disney's oldest traditions: We were waiting for Mickey Mouse to arrive on the train with his friends to "open" the park gates. Except we were already inside the park gates. Three generations, hand in hand, the Florida sun barely above the rooftops of Main Street U.S.A., music spilling into the air like a promise. Both the children's eyes went wide when the train whistle blew, and one squeezed my hand hard as Mickey stepped out, waving his gloved hand like he knew her personally. In that moment, I saw the little girl inside my daughter too. Her eyes widened and I saw the little girl who I had only been able to take to local carnivals, never to places like this. The little girl in her came out, the one that had been there before life made us both so serious. Her smile was worth a million dollars.

From that moment, the day unfolded like a true fairy tale. Our Disney guides took us to every classic childhood ride, no lines, no waiting. They dropped us at the ride entrance and took our stroller and belonging to meet us at the exit. My eldest granddaughter, who had laughed for the first time at Disney on our previous trip, seemed to bond instantly with one guide. She calmly and happily reached up to take her hand and chattered away as if she'd known the guide her entire 3 years of life. It was so out of character for her, and so amazing to witness, like watching a shy flower suddenly open in the sun. I saw my daughter start to loosen up too. Her and her husband fell to the back of the group, holding hands, talking and smiling. I smiled, knowing this was the trip she had dreamed of and had planned. Meals were ready the instant we walked into restaurants, with extra napkins and baby wipes. We were all surprised at the level of service.

When we reached the It's a Small World ride, my favorite ride for the calm atmosphere, my eldest granddaughter leaned over the front edge of the boat, her eyes bigger than saucers, even bigger than dinner plates, as she took in the bright colors, the tiny moving dolls singing in every language, the twinkle of the lights on the water.

It was almost as if, at 3 years old, she remembered riding it as a baby and some piece in her heart remembered her earlier trip as a baby when she had loved the ride. Even then, she had been spellbound by its slow, gentle rhythm, the unending chorus, the way every face of each doll no matter the location seemed to be smiling right at her.

This time, her little sister sat beside her, clapping in time to the music, both girls' laughter mingling in the air while their parents exchanged smiles that said:

"This is it. This is why we came: Memories are being made. This is the Magic."

I caught my daughter's eye while I was also watching them, and for a moment, we both just breathed it in, five lives connected in that little boat, all the years and angst between us folding away.

Later that day, Beauty herself chose our family to participate in her story time show. My son-in-law and the grandkids got to dress up as part of her enchanted wardrobe. And my granddaughter, the one who had once barely smiled, fell head over heels in love with another cast member who brought her into the spotlight.

She laughed again. And this time, it felt like the kind of laugh that heals something old. The kind of laugh that lingers.

We attended another VIP part of the park and watched a show unfold in front of us held on moving boats, we got sprayed by water cannons and had individual boxes of treats and goodies. Late in the evening, the fireworks spilled through the sky and laser light shined on the buildings.

For me, as far as I could tell, for my daughter that day was one of the happiest days on earth.

Selfridges, Socks, and Survival

London is a city where anything can happen, usually does, and dreams you did not even know you had can come true.

When I was still recovering from my broken back, I watched a series on Netflix about a department store in England: Selfridges. The story was about a self-made man, a visionary who seemed to at first get all the luck. I kept thinking, why did some people get all the breaks, and I only got broken? It was like a cruel joke the universe kept playing. But still, I was determined to go there one day. To walk through those storied doors, to touch something that felt like luxury, like a reward for surviving.

Eventually, the time came for the ultimate girls' trip, just my eldest daughter and me. I was preparing to move away to another country and wanted a great memory for us. We planned to go to England to see Platform 9 ¾, Harry Potter World VIP, the Beatles' Abbey Road, and a night bus tour of haunted places. Then to Paris for dinner in the Eiffel Tower, a river cruise on the Seine, a show at the Moulin Rouge for her, and Notre Dame for me.

I told my daughter we were going to Selfridges to buy socks. Just socks. That's what I said. Selfridges was so expensive that it was all I could afford, I joked. She laughed, not knowing the sock story was a smokescreen. In truth, I intended to purchase her a pair of Louboutin's. The red bottom $1,000+ heels she dreamed about. She had no idea. I used the sock story thinking socks would be near the shoes department, but of course, the shoes were on a whole other floor of this massive department store. Strangely enough, it was built by an American, full of elegance and extravagance.

We walked in, two modern-day Americans clearly out of place but pretending otherwise. She was naming off designers of clothes and luggage, demonstrating the confidence she always carried so effortlessly. I kept smiling, keeping my secret tucked close, trying to find the shoe department. Little did I know there were many shoe departments: each designer in its own store, on a totally different floor from where we were looking at socks.

We had been cherishing every second of the trip. She deserved this joy, this break from the world, as she had recently finished her college degree. Watching her look as if she were at home, watching her marvel at the world throughout the trip, made the trip perfect in my eyes. And we had not even gotten to Paris yet! I wanted her to know that for her, at least for this trip, anything was possible.

As we walked into the Louboutin store-within-the-store, there was a member of English royalty there that day: A very stuffy duchess. And believe me, she let everyone know. She was overly demanding with the female employee, and frankly quite rude to everyone in the store. A young lady was with her, clearly her daughter. Maybe 14 years old, a beautiful, cautious girl. Awkward with her long giraffe-like legs, still getting used to them and fumbling like kids do when they're in between childhood and adulthood. The mother insisted the employee bring her daughter a higher heel, but when the child stumbled slightly, the mother turned on her with that sharp tone only the elite can wield, berating her for not being able to "walk properly."

When we entered, the duchess looked at us and we definitely got the "oh, Americans" look. It had just rained outside, so our own shoes were wet. We were cold from the rain and not properly dressed for an extravagant and expensive shoe store. As far as my daughter was concerned, we were just looking and taking pictures to share with her friends, so what did we care?

When the male employee came up and asked my daughter what she was looking for, he immediately connected with her. "Would you like to see something particular? Will they be your first Lou's love?" She replied, "I am just looking. I love them all, but we are just looking and taking a few pictures to show friends at home." He nodded agreeably and offered, "Well, let's try on something anyway?" I felt that he knew we were not the type who could afford $1,000+ shoes, but he was beyond kind. He was also trying to avoid the duchess he whispered to us later.

He looked my daughter up and down and said, "I will bring the classic '**So Kate**' in a 3-inch and 4-inch, let's see how you like them."

She turned to the employee and gave an exquisite smile: "A 6-inch, please."

His eyebrow raised and he grinned with respect, saying, "This lady knows what she likes," as he headed to the back.

When she was fitted with the higher heel and the employee again cautioned her about the height. We overheard another short, biting remark from the "royal crew," the duchess once again criticizing her child. My daughter, age 24 and 5'7", stood up, even taller and more magnificent in those beautiful black, red-soled 5-inch heels. She stood gracefully, poised, elegant. She truly glided across the salon. It was a true "Pretty Woman" moment, as if she had been born to wear that pair of shoes.

She turned and whispered something to the child. I couldn't hear what she said, but I saw the expression on that child's face shift. A small, shy smile bloomed. A softening. Something was soothed in the child's soul. The mother gave a loud "HUMPF!" as she grabbed her items and the child's arm and stormed out of the store, the girl looking at my daughter as if she were the Queen.

My daughter returned to me with that same calm grace. We bought the shoes, we completely forgot about the socks. She carried that shoebox out of the Louboutin salon and down the street like a trophy. I carried that moment with me like a trophy. It was not really about the shoes anymore. It was about her. The very classy young lady she had become.

The trip was for her, but that moment? That moment was for me.

Falling Through the Sky

At fifty-something, weighed down by years of pain and despair, I thought this would be my final escape. No one would ever know it was intentional. I'd just unhook myself midair, and it would look like a tragic mistake. But I also told myself another story. The one I told everyone else. That I was jumping to prove something to myself, to face fear head-on, to show I was still in control of my life. Both stories were true in their own way.

As the plane climbed higher, my heart pounded—not from fear of the jump, but from the weight of what I was about to do. The cabin rattled with every shift in the wind, the smell of fuel sharp and metallic at the back of my throat. The instructor beside me cracked jokes with the other wannabe skydivers, laughing loud enough to compete with the engine's roar.

He wiggled his eyebrows at me like we were headed to a party instead of a leap into the sky. He slapped another jumper on the shoulder, telling some ridiculous story about losing a shoe mid-jump. I barely smiled. My hands stayed clenched in my lap, nails digging into my palms. I wasn't here for banter; I was counting breaths, making peace with an ending no one else knew about. My ears popped as the air pressure shifted, and my stomach gave a slow, queasy roll. Every tick of the altimeter felt like a drumbeat counting down my last seconds. The smell of fuel drifted through the cabin, mixing with the faint scent of worn leather from the instructor's gloves. My palms were damp, my breath shallow. I kept my eyes fixed on the tiny, toy-like fields far below, telling myself I wouldn't have to look at them for long.

The instructor nudged me and said, "You ready to fly?"

His grin was wide, easy, teeth flashing white against the dim light inside the cabin. I gave the smallest nod, because my voice felt locked somewhere deep in my chest. Around us, the others were loosening shoulders, flexing hands, acting like this was just another day. One woman hummed under her breath; Another man tightened his harness straps with a casual tug. For them, maybe it was routine. For me, it was the edge of everything. The plane's windows framed slices of endless blue, and I wondered if this was the last view I'd ever see. The instructor tapped the altimeter and gave me a thumbs-up like we were about to ride a roller coaster. I wanted to tell him this wasn't fun for me. It was a ride I might not come back from.

The door opened, and the wind roared like a warning. The temperature dropped instantly, a cold slap that made my eyes water even before we moved. The noise swallowed every other sound, pressing against my eardrums until all I could hear was its relentless rush. My jumpsuit snapped and flapped in the wind, each tug reminding me that I was seconds from stepping into nothing. I was strapped tightly to the instructor, my lifeline and my cage. The ground below looked impossibly far away, and the sky seemed endless. Everything inside me screamed to let go, to fall away from the life that felt too heavy.

Then the moment came. We stepped into the open air. I could not reach the airplane step, so he shoved me out in front of him. The world disappeared into a rush of wind and speed. The sound was deafening. Like being swallowed whole by a hurricane. My skin stung from the cold air, my cheeks pulled tight, my lips trembling against the inside of my mouthpiece. The air ripped every thought from my head except one: This is it. For a split second, I almost forgot the plan. Not because I didn't want it anymore, but because the sensation was so consuming it left no room for anything else.

My hands searched both myself and the instructor, desperately seeking the latches that held us together so that I could drop free. My cheeks continued to pull back from the force, my eyes watered behind the goggles, and my stomach lurched upward as gravity released me into the void. The sheer force of the air, the endless blue above me, the ground racing up to meet me. It was terrifying and beautiful all at once. I felt the instructor's calm grip, heard his steady voice in my ear, a tether to this world I wasn't sure I wanted to stay in. My hands were failing; I could not find a single buckle.

Like other times in my life, something shifted: It was subtle at first, just a loosening in my chest, as though the air was blowing through the cracks in my heart and clearing out the dust. Somewhere between the sky and the ground, my body stopped looking for a way out. The raw panic gave way to a strange, electric clarity. For the first time in a long while, I felt something fragile spark inside me. Not joy exactly, but something close to it. Hope.

As the parachute opened, the chaos softened. The sudden jerk yanked us upward, the straps biting hard into my shoulders, and my stomach dropped like a stone before settling. My ears rang from the change in pressure, and the flapping roar of the chute gave way to a soft, steady rustle. The violent pull upward nearly knocked the breath from my lungs, but then, very suddenly, we were floating.

Suspended between heaven and earth, the silence was almost shocking after the roar of freefall. It was the kind of quiet that made my heartbeat sound loud in my ears. The air around us was cool but gentle now, carrying a faint smell of sun-warmed fabric from the chute above. My legs dangled freely, toes brushing invisible lines of currents in the air. The wind gentled. Colors brightened. The horizon stretched endlessly in every direction. I could see highways carving silver lines through green jungle, clouds casting shadows that drifted slowly across the patchwork city.

The instructor pointed out my island across the channel. I could see for miles in every direction. I could hear my own breath again. I realized I still wanted to fall—but not toward death. Toward life. I wanted to pull the ripcord on my own story, but in a way that meant living.

That jump wasn't just a thrill; it was survival. A raw, breathtaking survival. It became proof that even in the most reckless, hopeless moment, a shift can happen. Even when you think you're falling to your end, you might just be falling into a beginning. It was my dark plan unraveling into a new kind of strength. It was a moment that whispered: **You are stronger than your darkest thoughts**. When my feet finally touched the ground, the earth felt solid in a way I had never noticed before. I bent, scooped up a handful of sand, and held it in my fist like a trophy. The instructor was grinning and high fiving the others, but I just stood there for a moment, feeling the pulse in my wrists, the air in my lungs, and the truth settling deep inside me:

I felt alive. And I deserved to live.

Into the Deep Unknown

The pool water was cool on my warm body as I sat on the edge, legs dangling over the water. My fear was palpable.

The sun was sharp above me, baking the back of my borrowed wetsuit and the smell of old dive gear clung to everything. The dive instructor stood beside me in the water, checking my tank, mask, and buoyancy device like it was just another Tuesday.

It wasn't. Not for me.

I was fifty, and this was my first time SCUBA diving. I had completed the classroom work for my SCUBA certification. Excited, yes—but nervous. I had never done well with enclosed spaces, cold water, or anything that blocked my breath. I knew why, but I wasn't going there. Not today. I had recently moved to Cozumel with nothing but time and the ocean. The diving package cost $300 USD, and the pool session was included with my long-term hotel stay. Still, I nearly backed out. I wanted to do it, but I was scared.

It brought me back to a childhood memory. I had always wanted to be a "water person," even though I had never learned to swim well. Maybe it went back to the day my older siblings threw me into the river at Arroyo Seco, when I was about seven or nine.

I came up sputtering and gasping while they laughed at my ineptness and shouted, "Well, you gonna swim or not?"

After that, I never felt fully safe in the water. But as a child, it was still easy to dream—marine biologist was once high on my list. I'd spend hours picking tiny creatures from the tidepools along Monterey Bay. That little girl would watch the waves wash in and out, each cycle bringing either treasure or danger.

"You ready?" The voice of the instructor brought me back to the present.

No. I wasn't. But I nodded anyway.

He motioned for me to put the regulator in my mouth and signaled: Go down.

The cold water wrapped around me like a second skin—shocking, silent. Panic roared within me. No, no, no, no, no! I popped back up, sputtering. The instructor rose with me, scolding me that I could put myself in serious danger, possibly even die if I did that in the ocean. If only he knew that might have been part of the reason I was here. He gave the OK sign. I returned it with trembling fingers. *No, I am not ok!*

As we descended again, I went through my secret plan again, silently in the darkest place of my mind. The thoughts I hid from everyone. I could get myself all ready. I could learn to dive. Just needed to know enough to be able to get out on a big boat in deep water. I could let the ocean finish the job I had never been able to. I needed it to look like an accident. No longer willing to just kill myself, I needed it to look not like a suicide. I needed my daughters to never think that I left them. I loved them. I could not pass any pain to them in my own cowardice.

The instructor touched my arm. Being underwater wasn't like I expected. Not at all. Underwater, there was no music, no cinematic drama like a movie. Just silence and the sound of my own breath—loud, steady, mechanical. I focused on it, on the way I had practiced. Inhale through the regulator. Exhale slowly. Watch the bubbles rise. But I was already fighting against going to the surface again.

The pressure hugged my ears. I was told to equalize, pinching my nose and blowing gently.

The water was blue, because the pool walls were blue. Nothing like the crystal clear blue teal turquoise color I viewed every day from the balcony. I wondered if I would really like to be in the ocean: A chance to see the famous coral cliffs, delicate fans, neon fish. I had seen them from the boat: Brilliant colors so impossible. Yellows so bright they looked painted, blues that felt deeper than language and greens that made grass on a golf green jealous. Schools of fish moved in choreography, weaving around as if they did not have any care in the world. For a moment, I was just a body in water. Breathing. Watching in my mind the beauty of this island. My eyes filled with saltwater. Not from the chlorine of the pool, but from something inside me. I let the tears come. Down here, no one could see my face.

I broke inside. I was in an absolute panic. Fear, Anger, Disbelief, Shame, Disgust. Each emotion had a name and they all fought to see which was stronger. How could I even consider ruining something so beautiful with my stupid silly ideas of ending my life?

The instructor pointed ahead: mask change drill. I signaled "WAIT" and stayed where I was, holding space for myself, maybe for the first time ever. What had I missed, all those years of managing, mourning, and believing I'd failed at everything? What if I could start over, go back and do it all again?

I pictured myself being 6 years old, sitting on the California coast shoreline for hours. I used to hold my breath underwater and imagine myself as a diver. Somewhere along the way, I'd let the world strip that wonder away, and the world told me to grow up. To let go of wonders and dreams. To prepare for what life demanded. And I had done that. I had done my duty to my family of origin, to my children, to everyone but myself. I wore the grief of my lost hopes and dreams and each of my failures like armor. I was Efficient. Reliable. The strong one. My inner failures were just known only to me. The weight of the world was closing in on me, just like the weight of the water. Instead of feeling hugged safe and secure, I felt like I was being held down by every failure of my life.

I panicked, my lungs screaming for air because I had forgotten to breathe from the apparatus. Without my permission, my body shot upward. Breaking the surface felt like waking from a nightmare.

"Where were you?" the instructor demanded. "In diving you have to BE HERE: In the moment! Mistakes equal death. That's enough for today. Let's try again tomorrow."

I sat alone at the pool deck, towel over my shoulders, wind drying my face. There was no reason for me to continue. I knew I was not the strong swimmer this sport demanded, and it was prohibitively expensive beyond my budget. I knew that I would never get to the point where I could take my own life. Another failure. What I had just learned reinforced that I belonged in the boat, on the water, the rhythmic, rocking movement of the sea is what I craved and sought from the ocean. I did not belong underwater, and I did not belong under the weight of things that had occurred in my life.

The attempt to dive hadn't transformed me, it had humbled me. Shocked me into remembering that I was still capable of being surprised. Of being small in a world that stretched far beyond my sorrows of failure: It is not always about me. My "need" to leave my pain behind could wait, I could carry both my grief and failure along with this new permission with me from now on. I could give myself permission to carry it, rather than weighing me down. I had the permission to let it go, when I was ready. To feel wonder again. To be a beginner. To breathe.

That afternoon, back in my hotel room, I rinsed the stench of the pool and the borrowed wetsuit and other gear from my hair, wrapped myself in a towel, and stood on the balcony. The sun poured itself over the Caribbean Sea, creating a perfect shade of teal turquoise blue green that no one could match in a paint color store. One that only can be found in nature. That perfect color I began to call "mine." I felt no need to check my phone, no need to explain myself to anyone if the day was a success.

I had gone down into the deep and come back whole. And I never even got below 10 feet. I never tried Scuba again. It had already taught me what I needed.

And maybe, just maybe, this thing called life? Yeah, I was definitely ready to try that again.

Transformation Through Migration

The first time I traveled to see Monarch butterflies, I was around eight years old.

It was fall in Pacific Grove, California— "Butterfly Town," the signs said. It started as just another chilly Monterey Bay morning in a government-assisted housing complex where windows stuck shut and walls were too thin for secrets. On cold morning drafts found cracks and on rainy days we brought out buckets and pots and pans to catch the water. I was looking for something healthier than 2-week-old packaged sweet hand pies gleaned from the bakery to eat.

I was the youngest of eight children. My mother worked at the elementary school I attended, as a teacher's aide, preparing classes sometimes before the sun came up and usually long after most kids had gone for the day. You could find her in the office, cranking the old mimeograph machine for the next week's handouts. I can still smell that ink and remember the purple stain it would leave on my hands as I helped.

That past week, as we printed the life cycle of the monarchs, my eyes welled up with tears. I still dreamed that someday I could go and see the famous groves. I learned from the worksheet that butterflies were not always beautiful. Only for a short part of its life would it have striking gold white and black masterpieces. They begin tucked away in eggs, emerging as ugly little caterpillars, and for a good portion they were hidden from the world in a cocoon. In that cocoon, they dissolved themselves into some kind of a butterfly soup, a goo of cells that when knitted back together, looked nothing like the original, but it retained their DNA . It would know how to get back to its ancestral home.

I knew, as well as I knew that cranky old mimeograph machine, that every year like clockwork, the monarchs came. I dreamt of seeing them as they floated through the eucalyptus groves like orange confetti from heaven. I had never gone to see the actual butterfly groves, as they were farther away than the city bus could take us. I was able to see the spillover: a few here or there, maybe a hundred at a time. Much as my hungry stomach was fed from the spillover of the local farm fields, a few tomatoes, celery, or lettuce here and there, sometimes more. My eyes, however, were fed by their stunning wings. I had no words to truly describe their beauty nor the feeling they gave me then—it was only that they made me forget I was wearing secondhand shoes and that they reminded me of something I didn't know I should have. Freedom. I just thought about those butterflies every year: They were free to come and go, keeping time with their long migration to and from places. They knew where and when they would go.I did not.Not yet.

But that particular day, someone came by last minute and invited me to visit the Monarch Sanctuary on a Girl Scout field trip. Another student was ill and could not go, so the seat was already paid. It was the first time I had ever been allowed to go so far from home unattended by my mother. I grabbed two more pies and shoved them in my pocket. There would be no lunch money I knew.

The Scout bus smelled like peanut butter and crumpled permission slips. I sat in an empty seat by the window, wide-eyed, no seatmate. It did not know anyone on that bus very well, even though some of them probably went to my school. I did not have the Girls Scout uniform, or the ability to go on the big events. Most of them were Junior Girl Scouts a little older crowd, I was just a Brownie Scout. I was not part of the clique even at such a young age. I didn't really know what to expect. I had never been on "fancy" field trips. As we began the approach to Pacific Grove, the eucalyptus trees were taller than anything I'd ever seen up close, swaying in the wind like something from a dream.

And then even from inside the bus, they appeared. At first one, then fifty, then a hundred. The famous Monarch butterflies. Thousands of them. Maybe millions. They floated in the sunlight like living petals, drifting between trees, flickering gold and orange against the sky. Some clung to branches in great clustered clouds. We left the bus, and some landed silently on the shoulders of my classmates. I watched them cluster in the trees, engulfing the trees so that it did not even show, just their wings flickering in the sunlight like stained glass. Some clung to leaves like folded prayers. Others drifted on the wind with no effort at all.

Little girl me whispered to them: *"Fly away! You are free! Go where I can't."*

At that time, many years ago, the butterflies at these groves were believed to be the same Monarchs that migrated as far south as Mexico City. The fir forests in Michoacán, Mexico would be the other side of the migration. Every year, the butterflies flew thousands of miles from California and Canada. Also from the U.S. Midwest all the way to central Mexico, to the same groves their

121

ancestors came from, but they themselves had never seen. I learned about the forests in Michoacán, so high in the mountains, thick with oyamel fir trees— where the monarchs gathered each winter, forming living blankets on the branches. Somehow, even though no individual butterfly had ever made the full journey, their lineage returned to the same trees. Generation after generation, they passed the migration route through their DNA.

I promised myself that one day, I would see the other end of that flight. Not just for them—but for myself.

Mesmerized, I watched the trees "breathing:" the term the scientists used for the movements of the millions of butterflies that completely hid the trees from view. I stood quietly on the trail, afraid to move too quickly, afraid I might scare them off—or worse, that I would wake up from my dream. I watched one butterfly spiral upward, turning in the light. It appeared to be leaving the swarm.

That little girl, so full of wonder and life for that one beautiful day leaned in and whispered to that solitary insect:

"Don't give up on me. I am going to see you there. Wherever you end up, someday."

I never got to visit the Pacific Grove Butterfly Sanctuary again. For that little girl with big dreams, it was all about survival. My older siblings had left home as soon as they could. Some didn't come back. I stayed close to my mom, trying to be the one that finished high school. As young as 8, I would be going door to door selling hand painted Christmas and Easter cookies and crocheted Christmas socks. I took part-time jobs cleaning and babysitting at 12 and full-time ones by 15 in fast food restaurants. Life had other plans for me and dreams are an expensive commodity when you are poor.

There was a move to Nebraska, then high school, the Marine Corps, community college, the endless night shifts, a scholarship that didn't even cover books. Marriage, children, all other dreams that were so beautiful and special to my heart. Meeting my needs in a million other ways, just as plentiful as a million butterflies. I was an adult and had to put away silly childhood dreams. I kept a list of those dreams patiently folded away in a book like the origami butterflies I kept. Throughout the years, I worked at Taco John's, Wendy's, Subway, Hardee's, a small country restaurant in a tiny town, as a mental health caretaker, a construction worker, a childcare provider. Living in Nebraska did not get me any closer to my dreams from childhood. But they never left my heart. That little girl was always with me, waiting for her turn to live.

On my 53rd birthday, 45 years after that visit to the California groves, I finally booked my travel from eastern Mexico to the hills of Michoacán. The journey was not easy: taxi, ferry, shared local transportation called a "combi," flight, taxi to a hotel. The next morning, I found a taxi to the local bus transport (like Greyhound) and took that to a small city in the mountains, then another public transport to the smaller pueblo of Angangueo, Michoacán. Somehow, I knew this adventure needed to be just me, not a tourist group as I had done with some others. I was not prepared, however, for the mountain cold or the oxygen-scarce air. The shuttle to the mountains of Michoacán was long, winding through villages with open-air markets and hand-painted walls. As they climbed higher, the air cooled, and the scent of pine began to fill the van.

The next day, I arrived at the gates to the sanctuary with a folding seat, my cell phone camera, and a tiny backpack for water. The air was excruciatingly thin after living at sea level for a number of years. My stomach trembled with excitement, nerves, and reverence. A small local taxi carried me the last stretch up winding roads

124

into the mountains of Michoacán. As they climbed higher, the trees thickened, and the light began to change.

On the way up, as I saw my first butterfly, I could not get the taxi driver to stop to take in the moment.

"Be patient, there's more," the driver laughed. "There will be more. No need to stop to look at just one."

He was so wrong: That first view was the one I needed. I felt the little girl beside me. She, too, wanted to have a conversation with that one individual butterfly. To tell it how she and I had both arrived.

When I arrived at the reserve, I could already feel that familiar hum, that sense of something holy. I chose to take a horse higher into the mountain as I was already starving for oxygen. Butterflies started to multiply, groups of five and ten, then groups of fifty, groups of a thousand…. And then I saw them.

Some were fluttering wearily; some seemed to be headed straight to the top of the mountain with determination. They had never individually been there, but they had instinct: A powerful, overbearing urge and need to reach where they were going, even if they did not know where that was. They reminded me of my struggle to become something more beautiful, and to find out where my urge and yearning would take me.

The guide explained how fragile they were, how few of the millions more never actually made it. How storms, drought, deforestation, and insecticides stole most of the population every year. Even when they had never seen the path. Even when the odds were stacked against them. And yet, still—they came. Somehow, they persevered. He also explained that these are not the same strain of monarch that I had seen so many years ago: with better technology they could better track migrations. It did not matter, however. I was not fulfilling the truth of science. I was fulfilling the dream of an eight-year-old who had finally made it here.

The monarchs poured through the trees like flame and silk. They clung to bark in dense blankets and lifted off in shimmering waves when the breeze stirred. The sound of their accumulated wings was almost inaudible, yet unmistakable. I closed my eyes to feel the heartbeat of the swarm. An actual flying raging river of millions of butterflies roared around me. It enveloped me. Never touching but surrounding me in eons of generations of historical passages. I stood motionless, tears slipping down my cheeks, I had finally reached my dream. I had reached the end of this migration. I realized that I had also morphed and changed.

I had waited a lifetime. They had gone through generations of metamorphosis: the one that flew away never returned here, and the one that left Pacific Grove did not return there. Maybe even thousands of generations over 50 years of insects dissolving into their own goo, becoming basically a butterfly soup. Then weeks later, a few cells that had remained unchanged become the memory of their ancestors. The cells remerge from the cocoon as that spectacular orange and black butterfly that could not even see the beauty of its own wings. I realized that I too could not see my own beauty.

One butterfly broke from the group and hovered near me. My hand, now wrinkled and sun-marked, lifted gently into its path.

And just like that long-ago day in Pacific Grove, I whispered: "*Gracias por no rendirte*." (Thank you for not giving up.)

Only as a child had I asked it: "Please wait for me."

I wasn't just talking to the butterfly. I was also talking to that little girl and to my adult self. Look at us: We *made it. We, too, are changed: but we are here*. The essence of us was here, even if the person had somehow changed. Just like the butterflies had morphed into something different from all those years ago.

That night, back in my freezing small room near the mountain reserve, I mentally journaled: Some journeys are too long for one lifetime. But still, we start them. And maybe, if we're lucky, we get to finish them too.

And if we are really lucky, we will be able to see the beauty in ourself without depending on someone else to see it for us.

The Sound of Silence

. During the height of the pandemic in 2020, Cozumel was not the vibrant island people remember from glossy travel brochures. The bright blues of the Caribbean still lapped the shore, but the life of the island: The hum of scooters, the chatter of shopkeepers, the joyful shrieks of children—had gone silent.

It was under what could only be called martial law, though few dared to use that word aloud. Streets once lined with mopeds, vendors, and the smell of fresh tortillas were now stripped bare. Police and National Guard vehicles patrolled slowly, like sentinels marking invisible boundaries. If you stepped outside, it was because you had a reason and that reason had better be good.

I had one: I was giving back. I had 30 families to feed.

Once a week, I was granted permission to leave my home. Not for leisure, not to wander the sea wall, but to make a lifeline run to the grocery store. My cart wasn't filled with treats or personal comforts. Instead, I pushed it down the quiet aisles, gathering despensas—bags of rice, beans, powdered

130

milk, oil, tuna, toilet paper. Basics. Sustenance. Enough to feed not just myself, but thirty families.

I had limited savings and a military pension check. They were not large, but they were more than enough for me. And now, I could stretch them out to be more than that.

Friends that I had met along my journey in Cozumel: Captains of boats, *Marineros* (Captain's first mates) and even the *sastre* (tailor) who had mended my clothing. I could return the kindness that they had given me.

Every week for three months, I went. I carried lists and baskets, my debit card slowly draining the last of my savings. What I bought wasn't glamorous, but it was life-saving—ninety days of children not going to bed hungry, ninety days of breath for parents who had wondered how to feed them, ninety days of food security.

Some families thanked me with tears in their eyes. Others, too proud to say much, gave a small nod, their gratitude folded quietly into the moment. I never asked for anything in return. What I gave was small compared to the weight they carried.

Many couldn't stay. Quietly, one by one, they left—taking ferries to the mainland, back to

Yucatán, Chiapas, Veracruz. They went where rent was cheaper, where hammocks swayed on grandparents' porches, where cousins would squeeze them under one roof. They traded the sharp teeth of an expensive island for the softer lean of family.

But some stayed behind. Some had nowhere else to go. One family, with no tourists to sell to and no jobs to return to, walked into the jungle. Day after day, they harvested coconuts—cracking them open with bare hands, pouring the water into reused bottles. They sold them to neighbors, to the rare driver passing by, and sometimes even to the bigger coconut vendors in town. It wasn't much, but it was survival. And survival, in those days, was everything.

I could not bear to leave the island. This was my home.

I was actually visiting in the USA on March 17, the day the world started to shut down. When we saw on TV that the Chicago airport was closing, we looked at each other:

You need to go get to the airport mom. She nearly whispered, reverently.

I need to go home before the airports close! I cried out, fearful of never seeing my island again.

The same thought, spoken out loud in fear of the future, at the same time.

One night, after making my deliveries, I sat in the stillness of my small kitchen and played The Sound of Silence—the version by Disturbed, raw and aching. Outside my window, the street that once pulsed with music, sizzling food stalls, and outbursts of laughter lay empty. A patrol truck rolled by, its lights sweeping the walls in rhythmic flashes, almost in time with the music. Not a voice. Not a step. Just the deep, unnatural hush of a world paused.

I walked out onto my little porch of that second-floor apartment to once again see with my own eyes do that I would never forget if we all lived through this. Again, I saw *nothing*. No cars, no children playing, the shops all shuttered. It was as dead as a cemetery at midnight.

Disturbed had released a haunting version of the song The Sound of Silence. Various people had taken that song and made COVID-19 versions on YouTube. Every time I watched these videos, I prayed that there would be future generations to show the video to. On the video it showed the same scene that was the lonely street outside my porch: Playgrounds, beaches, streets abandoned. Deaths from the Covid-19 numbers growing higher and higher, not only worldwide, but on the island. Scared people crying, searching for family members, standing outside windows of loved ones, not knowing what would happen.

4:17 seconds of haunting melodies. Paris, without a single tourist at the Eiffel Tour. London's Picadilly Circus without a single car in the roundabout and the London Eye empty. Wuhan, Milan, Sao Paulo, Madrid, The Vatican. Vacant. *!0,000 people maybe more. People talking without speaking*. The song wafted through the vacant streets of the entire world.

My sweet little Mexican street dog puppy was on the porch with me. Someone had brought her to me because the mother had instinctually killed most of the litter trying to save the last two. Hunger drove all of us to act in ways we would not normally. I had named her Corona (for the virus, not the beer) since she was born March 17, the day after I had headed back to Mexico.

Corona did not know the street was empty. She did not know anything except our tiny apartment, with slick tiles floors. She had never been for a real walk. Since all of the upstairs neighbors had left the island, we had the whole patio area to play together on. She never had felt concrete, asphalt or even grass beneath her feet. She had a fake plastic grass potty area.

I saw some neighbors' lights come on. Surprisingly, a few of them stepped out on their porches and patios. Some waved up at me. Some saw I had a puppy and asked her name. They all laughed when I told them.

Some who knew the english words to the song started to sing along. I played it 3 times, not wanting the distant camaraderie to end. It had been a while since I had interacted with people and been able to see their smiling faces. We were far apart, but there was friendship and kinship in that we were all going through this together.

As I spent time alone but yet together with my neighbors, I came to realize that my place on earth was right where I was supposed to be. Maybe I hadn't come to Cozumel for beaches or escape. Maybe I had been drawn here for this. This season of quiet giving, of filling a void in the middle of a global storm. I hadn't come to save anyone.

But I had stayed when other expats had left. I had opened my hands and when others closed theirs and walked away. Years later, those of us who were foreigners who stayed through Covid know each other. When others mention how long they have lived here or what they have given to the island, or that they consider themselves "Mexican" Or "Cozumeleño" we give each other a knowing look: *But you ran back to your home country when the going gets tough. Hurricanes and pandemics are enough to make you turn your back. This is NOT your "home."*

By the time the streets began to wake again, my savings were nearly gone. It had kept babies from crying from hunger. It had given parents a little more time. It had helped people discover strength they thought they'd lost. It also helped me make it through. It cemented my place on the island.

That kind of wealth doesn't sit in a bank account. But it lives in the soul.

Somehow, that silent, haunted street that had been patrolled, empty, heavy with the weight of those strange months became sacred ground.

Drowning in Perfect Color

It was meant to be a perfect day.

The kind of simple easy Island morning that tricks you into thinking that everything will always be just this type of perfect. I had worked for weeks to get *Mi Princesa* ready for days like this: scrubbing her decks until they glowed in the sun, polishing the cleats until they caught the light like little silver beacons, checking and rechecking the gear so nothing would steal from the joyous voyages I had planned. I was proud of myself for getting her ready: life vests, life ring, oxygen, anything that might be needed for an emergency situation. We could snorkel, dive, fish, I had her ready as a multipurpose boat. Today was just what we call a *paseo:* a pleasure day.

Porto Abrigo was quiet that morning, the kind of quiet you feel more than hear. Masts clinked in a lazy rhythm, and the smell of salt and diesel hung in the air. Birds called somewhere beyond the breakwater, the sound carrying in the stillness. My friend, someone I'd met just the day before, arrived with another friend of hers in tow. The three of us and my captain cast off into the channel of blue

138

water. Later there would be a rainbow of aquamarine, deep blue, sea foam, aqua, turquoise, teal, sky blue, blue green. Each perfect color complementing another and yet competing to see which one could beckon me to enter their warm depths.

As we motored north along the coast, the water started to become that living mosaic. Turquoise over the shallows, shifting into bright aquamarine, then deepening to a royal blue that hinted at open sea. Each time I looked away and looked back another color engulfed my senses. The sunlight was relentless, throwing silver across the ripples so the whole surface seemed to shimmer with some private magic. The low, steady hum of the motor blended with the slap of small waves against the hull, a rhythm as hypnotic as breathing. Every few minutes, a flying fish broke the surface, flashing silver before vanishing back into the depths.

I felt at peace, finally having convinced myself that just maybe, life was worth living. I was no longer in a suicidal place, and I was beginning to learn what it felt to be happy. It was as strange a feeling to me as a fish out of water. 50 years was all it took.

We passed the husk of an old, shipwrecked ferry, her steel belly torn open, rust bleeding down her sides. The salt-heavy wind carried the faint metallic tang of her decay. She had been claimed years ago by a hurricane. Wilma, a hurricane had left her there, lying part on the island and part in the sea. A Cozumel storm that arrived like a wall, tearing roofs from houses and dragging even heavy ships from their moorings. The ferry had been a beast in her day, built to haul people across the sometimes-rough water to and from the mainland.

Yet here she was, beaten, but still clinging to the shallows, the sea tugging at her bones but her strength kept them from finishing the job. 20 years she had been there, a reminder of what the sea made its own choices of who or what survived. Neptune had all the power, and he knew it.

The water around her hissed and lapped against her hull,

whispering stories of the night she broke. There was something almost defiant in the way she remained, as if she had decided that if she couldn't keep going, she would at least stay and bear witness. Every time I saw her, she reminded me of myself: Bent but not broken.

A few other boats were out that morning, mostly heading south toward the reefs or the tourist beaches. We waved as we passed. Those long, lazy island waves that are part greeting, part blessing, and part acknowledgment that out here, we all depend on each other more than we admit. I remember thinking how peaceful it all felt. Today the ocean was holding its breath just for us.

Our destination was a stretch of coast North of the island where few tourists go, a place perfect for snorkeling and swimming. The water there is so clear you can see the sand ripple on the bottom from twenty feet up, but the currents run like hidden rivers. It was a beautiful but deadly combination.

We dropped anchor and I dropped in first. I wasn't the world's best swimmer, I usually made the captain drop in first, but the day felt too perfect to argue that I was not the best test guide. I slid into the water. It wrapped around me, warm at first. I expected the gentle push of tide I knew from shore.

141

Instead, it hit me with the strength of a freight train.

The current slammed into my chest like a shove, quick and unyielding. Before I could even draw another breath, it was pulling me hard. Under the boat. Away from the safety of the ladder. My head broke the surface once, twice. Salt burning my nose, stinging my eyes, I was able to grab a breath before the water claimed me again.

I tried to shout, but he was already waving the other two women in.

"No!" My voice tore at my throat. "Don't let them in!"

But they were in. Laughing as they both dove. And then the current hooked them too.

The captain tossed a life ring. It arced wide and hit the water far too short. The sound of the faraway splash was mockery. My arms already ached from fighting the pull. The green beneath me turned to dark cobalt, deepening with every second.

I realized then where I was going.

The Cozumel channel. That strip between the island and Playa del Carmen where the water runs hard and fast enough to take a body to Cuba in just a day. People had died here. Many were never found.

The waves rose higher, slapping at my face, stealing breath before I could claim it. The taste of salt was everywhere—on my lips, in my throat. The boat was still anchored, the captain fumbling with the ropes.

A strange calm settled in. Maybe this is it, I thought. I didn't need to make a plan to leave this world; the plan had found me.

They say near-drowning brings surrender. Mine did. I let my body relax, I rolled onto my back, the water lifting me up as if I weighed nothing. The underwater hush wrapped around me, broken only by a faint rush past my ears. I told God I was ready. If He wanted to take me home, I would go without a fight. I was ready. I looked up at the beautiful sky, the clouds, the light blue that the water never really matched, and I was at peace.

Then came a scream. Sharp. Desperate. Needy. Terrified enough to pull me upright immediately. "AMY! HELP ME!!!"

"Damn," I thought, "I can't let *her die!*"

My young friend was close enough now for me to see the panic in her eyes. I shouted for her to stay calm, to relax and float toward me. The current had shoved me against some invisible wall. I was still moving but no longer carried farther out. She reached me, clutching at me like I was the last solid thing in the world. I shouted at her and told her she would drown us both if she could not calm down. We tread water together, desperately seeking the boat that was now too far away to see.

The third woman appeared, her strong, deliberate strokes cutting through the water. Miraculously, she had the life ring, the rope tied to her foot and trailing behind her. She was an open water swimmer, an ocean lifeguard and a triathlete. We each grabbed on like our lives depended on that little piece of plastic I had bought only 2 weeks ago. The three sets of shaking hands gripped the smooth cold hard surface of the life ring. We talked to each other, using breathing techniques to get enough oxygen back in our bodies. Calming each other down, doing anything to keep panic from swallowing us whole. Breaths came as ragged and quick as the waves had been.

Even though we were all scared to death, and literally holding on a life ring for our lives, I tried to joke:

"We will definitely be going to visit Cuba in our future if the boat does not come soon!"

In the area we had chosen for privacy, there were no other boats within sight to save us.

Finally, we heard the engine roaring to life far away. Its growl rolled across the water like a promise, even before we could see it. When we could, it felt like the boat crept toward us slower than a land turtle, closing the distance in slow, minute, aching increments.

When we were hauled aboard, our arms and legs were leaden, our bodies trembling. The captain assisted the other two women aboard and gave them oxygen. Me? Not even a glance. Not a word, not a hand to help me out of the water. Just another reminder that in my life, I was disposable to others who claimed to care for me. Rejected, I sat with my emotions: Now I know what facing death really feels like. God was not ready for me, I thought. I was so ready to face Him. I looked up. In a whisper, barely audible, I asked Him:

"Dude, if you have more in store for me, well will you get to telling me what it is?"

We made it back to port in silence, the sun slipping low over Cozumel's skyline. The air was heavy with salt, sunscreen, and the sweet smoke of someone grilling fish along the shore. Boats of all sizes and colors came together in line to enter the port. Scores of them, but not one knew the experience we had that day.

Something in me had shifted again. The woman whose fear had met mine in the water—she became more than a friend. She has returned to Cozumel several times since. We call each other soul sisters, because that day, in the space between life and death, we recognized the same truth: the ocean could take us, but it didn't. And that meant something. Something big enough to last. We still have that bond.

And as I stepped back onto the dock, my hand brushing the warm railing of *Mi Princesa*, I vowed to never allow that captain to touch me or my boat again.

Whales and Freedom

I was born in the Salinas Community Hospital and grew up in Marina, California, right on Monterey Bay. This bay is along the route of migrating whales of all types.

In school, each year we were taught to watch for the migrating whales. The bay opening is a place so wide and deep that when whales migrate North, they must come inside the bay for safety. The mother whales do this to keep their babies safe between themselves and the shore, so the babies don't get lost in the ocean. The whales communicate through echolocation, and the shore acts like a sound barrier, a natural guide between her and her calf. I never forgot that—how even the biggest creatures on earth, the California Blue Whale, still needed a kind of protection, a way to make sure their little ones wouldn't drift away.

When I was in elementary school, my class went on a trip to see the migration of whales. Again, a kind benefactor (a teacher) paid my way because my family didn't have the money. I was the youngest of eight kids, single mom, and we lived in government housing. Trips like that weren't just special, they were rare.

I remember the ride there. Everyone was excited, except for one boy, a refugee who came to California from Vietnam on a boat back in the '70s. He was the only one who got sick and threw up during the trip. I didn't know his story then, just that he looked scared and tired. That stuck with me—the way people carry so much inside, even when they don't say a word.

I was so excited just to be part of the group. I seemed to have natural footing on the boat when others did not. I could walk around freely, without falling or tipping with the waves. It was as if I had been born to be at sea, not on land. The captain spotted my sure footedness and allowed me to go to the upper wheel deck and it was then that I began dreaming of a career on the water.

The whales were incredibly larger and more magnificent than I had dreamed. They were huge yet graceful as they moved slowly through the water. I thought about how the moms must have felt, always watching, always protecting, their calves absolutely gigantic but still vulnerable. They were actual still infants. It was miraculous to see the baby given enough space to breach, to play, even be among other "tiny" whales, but under the ever-watchful care of its mother. I wondered again what I had done wrong in the world to deserve the amount

149

of physical and emotional abuse I suffered. The promise those whale calves carried was to keep the Blue Whales alive through their threatened extinction. Each had a place carved out for them in the world, even if they did not know their meaning. I thought about myself and where I fit in my family, how hard life could be, and how I wanted to become something more. What did I carry as a promise to the world, if anything?

I dreamed of escaping, of reaching higher. I wondered what it would be like to travel the streets of "Old Monterrey" in Mexico versus the New Monterey the Spaniards brought north with them. I dreamed of seeing the other side of the whale migration. Just like the butterflies in Pacific Grove, who traveled all the way to Mexico. I wanted to follow the path of the whales someday.

Years passed. Life and miracles came my way that I never expected. But that dream of truly seeing baby whales again stayed with me. Every few years, I would think about that promise to myself, but it was always the wrong time or there were no funds available, or I chose to take my daughters on a trip elsewhere. I knew in my heart it would happen…someday.

When I turned 55, I finally made it happen. I had moved to Mexico, and I had even gone to see the butterfly reserve in Michoacán. I was a different person now. Living on my own terms, the boss of my own life. No more being told what I could or couldn't do.

My mother was gone by then, but in my mind, I wanted to tell her something: "*Screw you, Mom. I made it. To the places you said I never would. Well, here I go again: On another trip you said I would never be worthy of.*"

My thoughts were not about anger. It was about proof. Proof that I could choose my path. Proof that I could fly as far as any butterfly or traverse any depth like a whale. Proof that somehow my life held value, and that I could find it. Proof that I had become myself, in spite of the years of obstacles.

I chose to go to Cabo San Lucas, a place one of my children had been on a church mission trip. There was a surety to see humpback whales and calves, California Blue Whales, maybe not.

Well, I said in my mind to little eight-year-old me: "Looks like this dream of yours gets a little tweak! But you're getting VIP this time—let's just pay and get the whole tourist shebang."

 Little ole me looked up at big ole me, laughed, and said," Come on, I'll race ya."

Within 20 minutes of boarding the tourist boat, there were a variety of humpback whales off the shore of Baja California Sur. Somehow, miraculously, a mother and baby showed up, and the baby breached. Once, Twice, up to 7 times. Just playing and enjoying the freedom of living. The naturalist assigned to the boat was snapping pics and video, amazed at what she was seeing. Soon the area we were in was surrounded by other boats. The spectacular creature breached and twisted like a gymnast on the pommel horse, throwing itself upwards out of the water again and again. Professionals were saying they had never seen such a show. I just smiled and knew that I came on the right day and the right time. That show was put on for me, but the others could enjoy it too.

His mother slapped her humongous tail and fins, and he followed suit. I watched in awe as this baby played, as if showing how safe he felt. He knew exactly who he was and what his future purpose would be. That baby was strengthening itself, testing itself, getting ready for a long and sacred journey of migration where it would take its place in the walk of time and eternity. One day he would be ready to make the trip back on his own. After he had grown and matured and experienced many things.

In that moment, another level of safety and trust unlocked inside me. Somehow, I knew I was on the right path. Just as these majestic beings were preparing to take theirs. I realized that all my trials were starting to drift away, like the boats returning to the bay. I felt safe. I had made it this far: Alone, without the help of family, friends, or partner. My own money, my own planned trip, my own choice.

"Look at how far you have come!" I said to 'little girl me' who was always at my side.

But she was no longer there.

"You did it!" I heard her whisper. "You do not need me to show you the way anymore."

Standing there on the water, watching the whales breach against the horizon, I finally started to feel free of my past.

I hope I continue to make that little girl proud.

The Little One That Didn't Look Back

There's always been something about the sea that called to me—not just the water, but the life that stirs beneath it. From the time I was young, I had a quiet dream written somewhere deep inside my heart: To see baby sea turtles hatch and make their way to the ocean. It wasn't something I talked about often. It lived on my bucket list like whispered hope, something that seemed almost too magical to plan. I didn't know how or when it would happen. I just trusted that someday, it would.

Years passed. Life happened. Some of it hard, some of it beautiful. Eventually, I found myself in Cozumel, a place that had become a kind of haven for many before me: An island full of color and contradictions, where tourists come for the sunshine and locals carry a history far deeper than the waves.

One day, a friend from Nebraska came to visit. She brought with her someone special. A kind, gentle elderly man under her care. He had developmental disabilities and a childlike heart that noticed things the rest of us often missed. His presence was simple, pure, and healing in ways unexpected.

We decided to join one of the more "touristy" turtle release programs—not the remote conservationist ones hidden in protected coves, but the kind meant to raise awareness, involving families, school groups, and yes, folks like us. It felt right. Accessible. Joyful.

We gathered on the beach at sunset, the sky painted in dusky pinks and soft lavender. The conservation workers carefully opened a protected nest and explained how these things go. The baby turtles near the top, still drowsy from the warmth of the sand, would soon wake up and pour out like red ants when water was in the hill.

And sure enough, they did.

Dozens of them began to stir, then scramble, awkward and determined, drawn by the scent and vibration of the sea. Drawn to the light of the moon over their new watery home. There was an explosion of tiny flippers and instinct. People clapped. Cameras flashed. Children cheered. It was beautiful chaos.

But in the middle of that wonder, I noticed something.

A single baby turtle lingered behind. His movements were slow and uncertain, his head bobbing slightly as though he wasn't quite sure which way was forward. He looked fine with no apparent injury, nothing seemingly out of place. He was just slow. Hesitant.

I watched him for a moment, quietly worried. Anxious that he, like me, would take the wrong path in life. I wanted to pick him up and put him on the right track, against his own will, as I am sure my guardian angel wanted to many times with me.

 And then I noticed our special friend watching too. He'd been distracted all afternoon, confused about where he was and why he was there, wanting to get back to the vehicle and go home. Not to the house, but back to Nebraska, where things were comfortable and he knew where he was and what to expect. He also was set on a different path this week. But right now, he was perfectly still. Intent, focused completely on this one tiny turtle.

He didn't speak. He just watched.

Five full minutes passed. That may not sound like much, but when someone like me who rarely sits still offers a newly hatched turtle my full presence for five sacred minutes, it means something. My friend also stood there with a quiet

156

kind of reverence, watching as the turtle paused, shuffled, rested... then tried again.

And then, finally, the little one reached the edge of the surf.

What happened next was subtle, but unforgettable. The turtle, once awkward and unwieldy on the sand, suddenly found ease in the water. He glided forward, fluid and fearless, letting the waves carry him home. He entered the water willingly without hesitation, no looking back.

I've been that turtle. I have hesitant, confused, weighed down by not knowing everything that was necessary to get where I need to be. There were so many seasons in my life where I didn't move forward because I wasn't sure if I could. Where I stood at the edge of something better and questioned whether I deserved to go in. I've been stuck in the sand. Tired, unsure, slow to trust that the water would carry me to a beautiful life if only I could get there.

But watching that baby turtle let go and swim, free, unburdened, a whole new future in front of him. It felt like that little girl me was again near me. Whispering directly to me:

Don't look back to the shore. You are in the ocean where you belong. Live!

I have made it through things I didn't think you'd survive. I am still here. It's time to trust myself. Time to step into the life waiting for me. Not all the lives I have lost, not the versions of me that were not worthy. Not the one I dreamed of, but the one unfolding right now. My life is full of mystery, grace, and second chances.

Our friend came up beside me, still silent, and gently took my hand in his.

He didn't say anything. He didn't need to.

In that quiet moment with the waves lapping at the shore and the light fading into night I knew we were all going to be okay. Me. Him. That turtle. My family. The version of myself I was slowly becoming. We were going to make it after all.

Not because anyone of us knew the way.

But because we trusted the tide.

Far Above the Ruins

It was still early enough that the world hadn't woken up completely. The interstate had been nearly empty; five lanes of traffic into the city would normally be full by now. Dew clung to the grass and the dirt roads, glistening in soft gold, and the horizon yawned open with just a hint of pinkish-lavender light. I stood, alone and quiet, on the edge of a wide, open field, nervously watching the *globos aerostáticos* (hot air balloons) of all sizes and colors—being inflated.

This day trip to Teotihuacán, Mexico, had started two hours earlier from Mexico City. It was freezing cold in the mountains, something I was no longer used to since living in Cozumel. As they called off names and balloon numbers, I began to think I had gotten scammed. My arranged driver had dropped me off and left. I had no contact name or ticket. Well, at least I got this far! Eventually, they called my name, and I found the balloon to which I was assigned.

It was fully inflated, and I was the last one to join the group. The ground crew was holding it back, leaning into the ropes with all their weight. I struggled to get into the gondola basket: 54 years

160

old, no longer as agile as the younger adults waiting on me, they were anxious to be the first to start today's voyage of approximately 100 beautiful hot air balloons. Eventually, they pushed me up and pulled me over, and I tumbled into the basket. Very grandmotherly and ladylike... NOT!

"Chicos," called the captain of the flight, "here is what you need to know, ok chicos?"

The balloon rose slowly, tugging against the basket like a living thing eager to be set free. Flames roared above as the pilot adjusted the burners, their sound both powerful and strangely comforting. The other passengers, all younger, seemed to be two combined groups. It didn't matter. I was there for my own experience, wanting to absorb as much of this day as I could.

One couple, a mother and daughter in her twenties, took selfies with ease. It reminded me of myself and my daughter in Paris. Another man, probably in his forties and the father, answered questions from the group with the excitement of a child. It wasn't his first flight, but for his family it was. My Spanish still wasn't fluent, and I tried to drown out the chitter-chatter. I was caught between wanting to film everything and wanting to be totally in the moment. I did not want to miss a thing and I also wanted to watch the videos because I was in disbelief that I had gotten here.

Then, without ceremony or notice, the ground began to fall away. I felt it in my stomach—not a drop, like in an elevator or roller coaster, but a gentle lift, like the hand of something unseen and kind. The gondola shook; the others laughed.

"Hang on, be careful, *abuela (grandma)* do not fall out!" someone teased.

I glanced below. The ground crews grew smaller. Trees took on the look of broccoli tops, and the small-town streets turned to delicate ribbons. Dogs, jumping and barking in yards, looked miniature. The catch trucks for the balloons looked like Hot Wheels. An area of farmland resembled a Triscuit cracker.

I didn't realize I had not taken a breath until the silence wrapped around me. Not silence exactly, but stillness. No engine, no honking cars, no phone ringing. Just calm. In fact, until the propane was opened again, I had never heard such perfect silence. There was just quiet and sky. It was completely different from skydiving or parachuting. The peacefulness and calmness were utterly dissimilar.

I looked out and suddenly felt like I was standing outside of myself—outside of any hurt, anger, and pain that I carried—outside of my memories, outside of time. The horizon curved gently. The sun now crested fully, sending light washing across the sacred pyramids of the Sun and the Moon at Teotihuacán. All soaked in gold. I blinked, and for one of the first times in years, my eyes welled up with happiness.

It wasn't the view exactly. It was the unassuming permission to feel small. And in that smallness, to feel free. It was permission to fulfill another dream, by my choice, in my way.

"You okay?" the pilot asked, his voice for the first time that day calm and casual.

"Yes," I said, my voice cracking slightly.

"Yeah, it does that sometimes," he smiled knowingly. It was the only two sentences that came out of his mouth that day that did not begin and end with the word Chicos.

The balloon floated over a group of tourists just starting to make their trek up the Pyramid of the Sun and others going to the Pyramid of the Moon. They looked up curiously, running, pointing, excited to see scores of balloons overhead. The early sun danced across the surface of other balloons. Each one rose and fell among the current. A smiley face one here, a rainbow, one in my favorite colors of the ocean. The floated up and down in and out gracefully with all the majesty of a ballroom dance floor. Each on its own path, but somehow all together. I saw birds below us, their wings slicing through air like paper planes.

I noticed the young couple leaning into each other, quiet now, phones forgotten. They were engrossed in the flight and each other. The man in his forties was no longer asking or answering questions. He just stared, open-mouthed, like he too was caught up in something old and precious. Something older than time. I wondered if the ancients of this area had once looked up and seen something or someone floating above these pyramids.

Floating here, above that sacred area of Teotihuacan , with nothing under my feet but a basket and the quiet trust of heated air above, I realized I had rarely risked seeing real wonder in my life. And I was grateful to myself. At least just for today.

My little me was pretty happy to, dancing around in my brain.

I had planned everything in my life. Tried to control everything I could. But this balloon? It went where the wind decided. It was an act of trust. It was surrender—something I was never good at, knowing that the rug could get pulled out at any time. That's what moved me most.

I looked over the side again, down to the earth so far below. "I'm afraid of letting go," I said softly, only to myself.

"Do it!" said little girl me. *"I am learning how and it's a ton of fun!"*

Eventually, the pilot pointed to a clearing ahead. "Chicos, we'll be landing soon. Might be a little bumpy, chicos." Honestly, I was so tired of the word chicos. Any direction, instruction, or comment from the balloon operator began and ended with that same word. It interfered with the solemnness of the occasion.

I didn't want it to end. For the first time in decades, I had nothing scheduled, nothing expected, and nowhere to be. Just sky and wind. Just to be. And right now, that was here.

The landing was gentle—two small bounces, then stillness once again. The crew quickly started hollering out instructions to deflate and pack up the balloon. The magic was broken. As the others took group pictures, I just stood and stared at the basket, realizing I was still warm from the fire. It hadn't changed anything—not in the way dramatic experiences are supposed to. I still had to figure out how to get back to Mexico City.

Before today, I had done some crazy things: skydived, gone on a transatlantic cruise without anyone I knew, traveled to Scotland with someone I barely knew. Heck, I had even sold my house and "ran off," moving to Mexico alone! Safe to say my mid-life crisis was achieved.

But today, again, something inside had shifted. The sky had shown me how small I was in the big universe across time and space. In that smallness, how beautiful it all was. Maybe my life did hold meaning. Maybe it was okay to step out of the perfect prebuilt frame now and then. To let go. To be carried by something invisible, like a current. To feel the wind and not fight it.

And just maybe… that rug was not going to get pulled again.

I took one last, longing look at the balloon, then turned toward the waiting flatbed truck to join the others for breakfast, the sun now fully risen behind them. I walked forward with a new purpose. Not to escape my life this time, but to return to it, having seen it more clearly from the sky.

Dreams of Mexico Eclipsed

Not everyone can walk
away and find themselves.

As I planned to visit the
monarch butterflies in Michoacán,
watch baby whales off the coast of Baja California,
and visit Monterrey to fulfill childhood dreams, I
made a quiet promise to adult myself—one I hadn't
quite dared to say out loud before. I would visit
every single one of Mexico's 32 states.

I had fallen in love with this country head over
heels. The people, the food, the rhythm of life that
moves slower here, gentler somehow. My
American-style Type A personality was melting
away, piece by piece. No more was I demanding
and rushing. I was changing, softening, and Mexico
was quietly guiding me along that path.

This new dream was not just to see famous
landmarks or check places off a list. I wanted to
spend time to understand Mexico in its fullness. I
wanted to know the pulse of its cities, the breath of
its forests, the stories etched in its mountains and
rivers. How this country had been shaped so vast
and varied, and how it was shaping me in return.

On the eve of Independence Day 2023, I found myself in the heart of Mexico City at the Zócalo. Surrounded by a sea of over one million faces, mostly Mexican but of all nationalities, the crowd sang with one voice. Flags of green, white, and red fluttered everywhere. It felt as sacred as standing inside the very heartbeat of the nation. The following day I watched the parade of the military, and my heart grew once again. As the President of Mexico appeared and recited the Cry of Dolores, I could not help but join in the Viva Mexico, Viva Mexico, Viva Mexico at the end. So many shining, proud faces, both young and old. They had the liberty of serving a country that did not go to war with other countries.

Another voyage took me south to Chiapas. I stood before waterfalls so turquoise they looked almost unreal, watched streams shimmering like silk beneath the jungle canopy. The Lacandón Jungle welcomed me next—a vast, breathing green cathedral. It's Mexico's largest and most biodiverse forest, home to an astonishing array of life: 15% of the nation's plants, a third of its birds, countless butterflies that danced in the dappled sunlight. Deep in this jungle, I met a hidden tribe living in harmony with the land. Their clothes were woven from natural fibers; their lives entwined with the rivers and trees. They welcomed visitors with ancestral grace—not performances as seen in Xcaret, but an honest, natural way of being passed down through generations. True natives who have been here longer than time itself, they truly belonged to the jungle. That night, as the jungle sang its lullaby, I felt Mexico herself tucking me in, whispering, "You belong here, too."

Oaxaca, where the scent of freshly ground corn tortillas filled the air, and the colors of the markets rivaled the brightest rainbows, also called me. Here, ancient traditions breathe life into every corner, and the recipes of mole that take days to make but took hundreds of years to refine. In the same trip, I visited further north in Nuevo León, the rugged Sierra Madre mountains stretched out like a protective wall. I found solace in their quiet strength, a reminder that resilience often wears the face of patience. It was a reminder to stay steady in times of change. I finally made it to "Old" Monterrey and the little girl beside me smiled again.

"We really can make your dreams come true: Both our dreams"

The salty tang of the Gulf that reached clear to my last home in Mississippi mixed with the rhythms of music from open windows in Veracruz. The city's streets pulsed with life, a blend of African,

Indigenous, and Spanish roots that told stories older than memory

Another childhood dream of seeing the fearless cliff divers in Acapulco, silhouettes against the fiery sunset, launching themselves from dizzying heights into the dark waters below. Their leaps were both a dance and a defiance—a reminder of courage in the face of gravity and fear. They told me that they were part of generations of divers. In the same way I saw only the progeny of the butterflies, here I met grandsons keeping traditions of their sacred ancestry.

In the deserts of Chihuahua, I made a new promise: to return and travel on the train El Chepe through the Copper Canyons. Oddly enough, I did not see even one Chihuahua dog, namesake of the state! But it did have a sky so vast it seemed to hold the universe itself. I understood how solitude can be a balm. The silent expanses had me thinking of endurance, about the beauty of stillness and not changing while everything around me did.

I wandered through Guanajuato's labyrinthine alleys, where every corner seemed to hum with history and the walls whispered stories of revolution and romance. The city's vibrant colors and hidden courtyards invited me to lose myself and find new parts of myself in return.

In Puebla, the Chiles en Nogada and freshly baked bread filled the streets. The colonial architecture stood proudly beside bustling markets, a testament to the blend of old and new that defines so much of Mexico. It was the only state where three people asked me to take a picture with them for no other reason than I was white!

On the Pacific coast in Colima, I stood on a black sand beach, the volcanic grains warm beneath my feet, a newly purchased cowboy hat on my head. I was reminded of a George Strait song that had encouraged my move: The Beaches of Old Mexico. I had been following the footsteps of the man in the song: Juárez, then Durango, Colima, Almiera, Manzanillo, and here I was in a hammock on the seashores of Pascuales. It fit perfectly. I feel as if I laid the dream of my son that I never had to rest there on the Seashores of Old Mexico. My little shadow girl ran and played in the black sands, alongside me.

After each adventure, I returned home to the sun-drenched beaches of Quintana Roo, where the Caribbean Sea laps gently against white sands, reveling in the thought that each state I visited opened a door to a new chapter of Mexico's story— and my own. Each state offered a new layer—a different way to see, to feel, to become. I was no

173

longer just passing through; I was weaving myself into the fabric of this land, and at the same time, it was weaving itself into my soul.

A year later I flew to Torreón, not realizing it was right in the path of a major eclipse just a few days later. I walked among the dinosaur digs—ancient bones whispering stories of a world long gone, connecting me to a past as vast as the land itself.

I rode the *teleférico* (cable car) to the top of the mountain to see the Cristo de las Noas, also known as Cristo Rey. This Christ statue is 72 feet (22 meters). In Mexico, I also visited Cristo de la Paz in Zacatecas (33 meters). The Cristo Redentor in Rio de Janeiro, Brazil is more famous and stands 30 meters. I also viewed the Cristo Rey de Silao (20meters) in Guanajuato, and Cristo de Chiapas in Tuxtla Guiterrez, Chiapas during my travels. Today, however, the buzz was about something even larger. It was all around me, everywhere I looked: Eclipse, Eclipse, SEE THE TOTAL ECLIPSE. Connect with the ancients this April 8, 2024. It was posted everywhere.

I waited until the last minute on April 6th to decide to stay longer to see this once-in-a-lifetime occurrence. I stood, boarding pass in hand, and watched my plane fly away from the airport without

174

me. Something I would never have done in the past, but it was a step in learning to let go.

Finding a hotel room was the first step in the line of comedic and tragic events. The next day, the chance of fog sent NASA scientists—and me—scurrying west toward Jalisco. What a feeling it would have been to end my journey through all 32 states on the shores of Mazatlán, Sinaloa, beneath an eclipse, in the hometown of my favorite Mexican band, with literally hundreds of thousands of people on a beach.

But mishap after mishap blocked my route and my dream. I booked my bus online, got to the station, and the bus had not yet left Monterrey: It would not be arriving. There was no other bus to Sinaloa, but there was one to Durango and, if it all worked out, I could find another bus or a rideshare the rest of the way. Luckily, I was able to get a bus to Mazatlán. I would arrive in the morning around 9 a.m., and the eclipse would be around 2 p.m. Perfect. Then, my bus was involved in a wreck right at the Mazatlán/Durango state line, in the mountains, five hours from Mazatlán, and in a tunnel, of all places. I was beginning to think the universe was blocking my view of the eclipse. After arguing with the bus driver, I grabbed my backpack and left the bus. He would not allow me back on, he said. No worries, I will find my way: there are only four hours of traffic blocked up behind us! I walked out of the tunnel and stood in the quiet majesty of Durango's pine-covered mountains, feeling the cool air sharpen my thoughts. I could see the trail of cars, trucks, and people outside of their vehicles for miles.

Grateful I had bought some eclipse glasses before I left, along with some moonstone necklaces that I felt silly about putting into the beams of the sun, I climbed a small hill nearby. I placed my necklaces and some Christian amulets gently on the ground before me and removed my shoes, grounding myself in my own moment of disappointment. Do not let the things that happened before affect your opportunity today, I whispered to myself. You are here, safe, and you will see this eclipse, even if it is not how you had dreamed. Some dreams come true differently. You survived another wreck that could have killed you. Focus on the moment.

Then the sky began its slow transformation. The sun, which had been blazing bright, started to dim as the moon inched across its face. Shadows lengthened, and a hush fell over the travelers. Colors softened, the air seemed to hold its breath, and the world slipped into a strange, sacred twilight.

I was torn between being completely in the moment and the urge to take pictures to share the sacredness with others, especially my daughters. I knew the moment was fleeting and I wanted to remember every detail—those twenty-some minutes would pass in a second.

As the eclipse reached totality, the sun's corona burst forth—a glowing crown of light shimmering like a halo in the darkened sky. The temperature dropped quickly; a cool breeze stirred the pine, then it was still. Silent. I felt tears roll down my cheeks, not from cold, but from awe. Here I was, far from home, in a foreign land, caught in a moment that connected me to the vastness of the universe and the enduring heartbeat of this world. I finally saw and felt what the Aztecs and Mayans must have experienced: there must be higher power(s), because something this perfect must be by design—it could not be chance.

In that silence, I understood something profound: this was more than an eclipse. It was a symbol of cycles, endings and beginnings, darkness giving way to light. And in that fleeting, beautiful shadow, I felt deeply held, and I was deeply seen through time and space. In that moment, just a few hours away from ending my dream to put my foot in every state, I became completely Mexican.

Chosen

During my first year in Mexico, I owned a boat. She wasn't much to look at compared to the sleek, expensive yacht in the next slip, but she was mine. She had a few stubborn stains; her paint faded from years in the sun. To me, though, she was beautiful. I saw her in the way a mother should see her child, flaws and all, and loved her even more for them.

I spent most mornings in the marina working on her. Cleaning. Organizing. Making her feel cared for. I didn't know much Spanish then, and I often felt like an odd piece in a puzzle that didn't quite fit. Most boat owners didn't tend to their vessels themselves — they hired crews. And I was a white woman in a space that seemed to belong to men who had been working the sea longer than I had been alive.

In the slip beside mine sat a striking vessel — long, gleaming, everything my boat was not. The captain was always there, working with an easy rhythm born from years on the water. Every morning when I arrived, and every afternoon when I left, he'd acknowledge me with a nod, a smile, a "*buenos días*" or "*buenas tardes*."

179

"Call me Capi," he told me. And I did.

Capi had been there the day my boat was first lowered into the water, part of the group of captains and *marineros* (first mates) who treated the event like christening. They all were so happy for me. However, my own hired captain, when he bothered to show up, rarely did much. I started to work on her every day, usually alone. Learning in the processes, sweating under the sun, sometimes making mistakes I didn't even know were mistakes at the time.

At first, I was hesitant to ask questions. But over time, my neighbor at the next slip began offering small, quiet tidbits of advice when he saw me struggling. I'd ask why he tied a rope a certain way, why he used one tool instead of another. He would always explain in his quiet, simple manner, patiently, without making me feel foolish.

Our friendship grew in little moments. Sometimes the clink of a Coke or Dos XX bottle offered on a hot afternoon, the shared laugh over another of my mangled attempts at a Spanish phrase, my fumbled attempts to learn to tie another sailor's knot, the teasing splash of a wet sponge lobbed from one deck to the other. And especially me learning bad words in at least three languages.

Eventually, I left the marina, and the boast went to others. But the island is small, and I would run into my friend often. Each time, there would be a great big hug and a smile that could light the whole street. When circumstances allowed, there was a cold beer pressed into my hand and he would proudly say: "When you are with me, you do not pay. I PAY." Since I had been taken advantage of so bad, it was a point he made in front of everyone: He would take care of me. He would tell anyone who'd listen about "la Princesa" who worked her own boat, and I would praise him for his kindness in helping me adapt and keeping me safe from people who could have taken advantage of me. He began to tell others that I was his sister, as we never wanted a misunderstanding about our friendship in the world's eyes. He was the best brother I could have.

Over time, and mostly through him, I met more friends. Ones that did not see me as a bank, but as a true person, just like them, trying to live their best life. I learned where to get chickens for my yard, which fruit stands were best, what plants would grow well in my garden, and how the rhythm of the island wasn't something you mastered, but something you became a part of.

One evening, I met his wife and family. His children and grandson were close in age to my own family back in the USA, and we bonded quickly. They began calling me *tía*. The Auntie. It reminded me of when my nieces and nephews were younger, and they all called me " Aunt Amy."

I laughed when they teased me about surviving the hangovers they swore they would inflict on me during family parties. His wife nursed me through dengue fever by bringing over *sangre de cristo* (a beverage) and love. They would bring me fruit from their trees: Mangos so ripe the juice ran down my wrists, huayas that tasted like summer itself. The introduced me to the red hairy little fruit called Rambutan, and I fed them American style tacos.

Over many years, I have been enveloped and adopted by this family. I will never understand why or how we found each other, or how I was chosen by them. But in the quiet moments when I'm seated at their table, laughter rising around me like a tide, I realize it doesn't matter. I didn't know I needed them, but now I cannot imagine living without them. Though I live alone, I don't feel alone anymore. I've got a family here in Mexico who sees me, who gets me, who teases me about the next party and taking me to other states. A family who will mercilessly laugh at my terrible attempts at

Spanish idioms, *dichos and frases*, who explains their culture to me without judgment. A family I love back with every corner of my heart.

Families can be a lot like that: Like the sea, they didn't welcome me because I conquered them. No one could conquer that family. They welcomed me because, in their own quiet way, they decided I belonged. Some bonds aren't earned by deeds or measured by worthiness, or if the *Guerra* (white girl) has money or not. Some bonds are true gifts, freely given. Like the sea, they welcome you not because you have conquered them, but because, in some mysterious way, they have decided you belong.

This Christmas, in the year 2025, nearly 50 years from my earliest memories told in this book, we will celebrate as a family. I'm doing what most Americans would probably call a "back to basics" kind of holiday. There won't be piles of store-bought gifts, no big commercial spree. Instead, there will be homemade vanilla that I have been patiently creating for nearly a year, bottles found locally to fill with honey I've also sourced. Loaves of bread from a local artisan baker, and lots and lots of Dos XX, Jack Daniels, Rum, and Don Julio Reposado. I will host several different parties and just like last year they will be full of laughter and love. This year I am introducing the always-rowdy Dirty Santa game, with the presents all provided by me but the trading by the guests.

I will not have a typical Christmas tree as my house is tiny, and I have children here. But what makes it truly special isn't what's under the tree, it's who's around it. It's not what is in the package, it's who's holding it. **These are my people**. They are my family of choice, not by birth. The friends who have become woven into the fabric of my soul. *Mexico mi adopto.* Mexico has adopted me. Cozumel embraced me. And my new, chosen family has wrapped me up in something more precious than tradition: A family to belong to. This year, Christmas isn't about things. It's about vanilla, honey, belly laughs, beer and love.

It's about being *chosen.*

Dreams delayed, not Denied

When I was thirteen, my family packed up and left California. We were chasing something quieter—less expensive, less violent, less tangled in the chaos that California had become in the '80s. The drugs, the crime, and even the subtle hostility toward white families had worn us thin. My parents longed for a simpler life, so we migrated to Nebraska. The population of the small town we moved to: 214. To put that in perspective, my eighth-grade class alone back in California had 210 students.

During the 1,000 plus mile migration, I became ill. I had developed kidney stones as well as dehydration from the trip and needed to be hospitalized for surgery. We were a caravan of 3 vehicles, practically my entire family of origin, brothers, sister, babies, cats, dogs and maybe even a bird. I think we must have looked like the Beverly Hillbillies the way the vehicles were packed down. The emergency stop when I started urinating blood and vomiting was a kink in the plans.

My mother decided to leave me at the hospital and continue to their new home. I was left, completely alone, 200 miles from their destination.

185

I was not sad; I was in too much pain to understand or care. A few days later, strangely enough, I had never felt so free. I was catered to by the nurses and given "front row window seats" to watch the fireworks for the USA Independence Day Celebration on July 4.

The hospital was on the verge of calling social services to place me into foster care when my sister finally arrived to pick me up over a week later. My mother did not even come. I could see her disdain as the nurses explained that I could not be in the heat, have Air conditioning, and needed to take it easy for at least 6 weeks.

"Yor dumb ass was sure smart enough to figure out a way to get out of helping move and set up house." She growled at me in disgust as I got into her car.

We both knew that she would have rather left me there.

I was not a dumb kid, but I did not force myself to be ill. Contrary to the angry voices always calling me stupid, I was pretty smart. I had tested super high in IQ and ability tests at a very young age.

From 3rd grade on, I had been placed in gifted classes. I thrived on challenge. I loved learning, loved asking big questions, and I loved that teachers expected something more from me. It was often a way that I was nurtured, and people actually cared what I had to say. I attended one school from PreK to 6th grade and had read nearly every single book in their rather large library. I also read the encyclopedia set that we owned and always moved with us to our various homes. When we moved, I always found a place where I could hide out and read and keep my pulse on the mood of my mother. I was always hiding in a corner, reading, hoping no one would notice me. When she called my name, I would immediately be there. I knew better than to not be within voice distance. Whether it was just to get her a Diet Pepsi or a favorite Black Cherry Cola, I was there. Sometimes it was to go to the store for a chocolate candy called Ice Cubes. You better be sure I would run all the way back so that they did not melt. I made that mistake. Once.

But here I was in a whole new world, something I had never even imagined.

In Lawrence, Nebraska my world changed overnight. The 5 students in grades 5 through 8 were lumped into one basement classroom of the high school. I remember walking in and thinking: Is this real life?

It felt like I'd stepped into another century. I begged my mother to move to a bigger town, and two years later, after my sister had moved North, she relented. It had nothing to do with me however: She could not drive, never had learned, and we did not have a car. My brother had left for the US Army, so it would be easier for her to get financial help, food stamps, and to get a low-income apartment in a city.

But arriving as a geeky brainy junior moving into a clique town in Hastings, Nebraska where everyone had grown up together? I didn't exactly blend in there either. At least I could get lost in the population: Again, there were 200 kids in my graduating class.

I was quiet. I didn't try to participate in sports. Not because I was lazy, but because no one had ever taken the time to teach me how to play them. I didn't fit into the basketball-and-volleyball jock crowd. I wasn't fashionable, wasn't flirty, didn't know how to work the social angles. I did not drink or use drugs either, so I did not even fit in with the outcasts.

Also, I needed to work. I worked after and even before school at various fast food restaurants, sometimes walking 4-6 miles a day between school, home, work, home. I pretended that it did not matter, that I just wanted to learn. It was easier to not try and fit in. I could not bring friends home to the atmosphere I lived in.

Most of the students in high school were enjoying their youth, and social status. Many already knew what college they would attend. So many other kids were just blowing off their classes, cheating, and ditching class. I could not believe people would waste their one opportunity to get an education! I took eight classes a day but no study halls to keep me occupied but I wasn't happy. In reality I was beyond lonely.

Senior year, I found a little escape. I enrolled in some community college classes in the afternoon. Not just to get ahead, but to get away. Away from the cliques. Away from the judgment. And with students who were paying to be at school, there was real interest in what they were learning. I felt as if I was finally a part of a crowd, that my opinions actually mattered. And the Pell Grant money helped, too. It didn't just cover tuition; it helped support my mom and me. I was still working too, but heat and food and rent were expensive. I thought about college. A real university. It felt out of reach.

I couldn't even scrape enough money together to afford to take the ACT or SAT. No one at the high school or the community college told me it would've been free for allow income kid on the school lunch program, or on a pell grant. No teacher, counselor, or advisor stepped in. I gave up my childhood dream of becoming a veterinarian. It wasn't that I didn't want it. It was that I didn't think I could have it. I stayed at community college until I graduated high school.

There was a small party, one I paid for myself, and some family members came by. My mother told me that day that it was time to pay half the bills or move out. I guess she did not realize I already was.

I moved in with a boyfriend. I hated it. I was looking for more than just to be an old-fashioned spouse who put food on the table and kept the place clean and spit babies out. I had a miscarriage, and he blamed me, and threw me out. He had not even told his family, even though I was 4 months along. He showed me, like so many others, that if I did not live up to his standards, or provide what I was told, I was worthless.

I tried to go live with my father for a short period of time, but our lives were just too different: He expected a quiet, polite little girl, and I had been a fighter my whole existence. Once again, I was left to take care of someone else while the adults did their own thing. He did help me get a car, that I had

190

to pay for myself, so once again, instead of studying, I was working.

Eventually came the opportunity to enter the Marine Corps. I had been throwing the idea around in the back of my head. My Marine Corps brother, home on leave, had gotten himself in some trouble with the law. He needed a couple weeks to get it figured out before he went back to his duty station. His recruiter signed me up, saying my brother was his assistant, which gave my brother 30 more days of leave. I guess it worked out for everyone.

In the military, I finally found something I'd been missing: a place to belong. I didn't care about college right then. I cared about doing something meaningful, about being part of something bigger than myself. I wanted to be the best Marine I could be. I threw myself into my MOS school in the daytime, took some classes in college at night, and was chosen for several honor situations. I just fit in.

Again, I was still sending home most of my paycheck to support my mother and some of my nephews and nieces. I was literally getting paid $17.50 twice a month. I did not care: I had a bed, food, and clothes for work. I was not off duty much, so I only needed a few civilian outfits. These were the best days of my life! For once I was not focusing on surviving, I was thriving!

But once again, the rug got pulled out from under me. A medical discharge ended my military career under honorable conditions, but it sure felt like failure. I was ridiculed by my family.

I ended up back in Nebraska. I dusted myself off and went back to the community college using a Pell Grant, this time hoping to get a job at the local WIC office. I wanted to teach families how to eat well on a budget as much as I wanted a job where I could keep an eye out for kids like me and try to get them some help. I wanted to make life better for others, even if I had not known how to do it for myself.

Then life threw its hardest punches.

My child died. Then two more high risk pregnancies and both babies came prematurely. Suddenly, I was divorced and a single mom. The university dream was off the table again. I poured my heart into my daughters. I told them: College is not optional. You will go. You will learn. You will have what I never had.

And they did. Through my veterans' benefits, I helped fund their education. I couldn't build my own dream, but I could help them build theirs.

Years passed. Seasons changed. And somewhere in the middle of all that, I found myself in Cozumel. I had planned to travel until my soul began to feel at rest. I noticed that the island of Golondrinas (sparrows) and the Mayan Goddess of Abundance Ix-Chel were doing just that. Giving me a place to rest.

For the first time, life slowed down. The pressure eased. The world grew quiet enough for me to hear something I hadn't heard in years: My own voice.

And little girl shadow beside me started bugging me again: Can we go see the butterflies? The whales? Why did we not go to Old Monterrey yet? *Can we get a bachelor's degree?*

I knew she was pushing me to start fulfilling our life dreams.

I enrolled at Southern New Hampshire University. Online classes. Late nights. Quiet mornings. I earned my bachelor's degree at age fifty-six. It wasn't the degree I'd first imagined, straight from high school taking on the world. Life felt like it had taken a huge detour, a bend in a road I hadn't expected to be so long.

Through it all, imposter syndrome trailed me like a shadow, whispering that maybe I didn't belong here, that maybe I still wasn't enough. I knew what imposter syndrome was throughout my entire life: the feeling of not being worthy of your earned and rightful place in life. College had given it a name, but the feeling was already very familiar. It was probably my best friend.

Still, I kept going. I pushed through semesters that sometimes felt like they'd never end, chipping away at assignments between the rhythms of my new life in Cozumel. I had "retired" there, but it wasn't the kind of retirement people imagine. It was not the end. For me, it was a new beginning. The ocean stretched wide and steady before me, the pace of life slowed, and I found space to dream again. I wanted to prove to myself that it wasn't too late to learn, to grow, to accomplish something that had waited far too long.

Some classes were harder than others. Statistics terrified me so much that I took it through a different online platform first, just to ease the fear before facing it head-on. To make sure I didn't fail, I took it through Sophia Learning first, easing into it on my own terms. Little by little, I crossed the finish lines of each course, until, one day, there it was: my degree.

Someone once told me, "You throw great parties for others! Why do you never have a party? Why not for yourself?"

Well, it was because of my best friend Imposter Syndrome: I did not deserve it like others did. BUT WHY NOT? *Entonces,* (therefore)I threw one. Not a polite little gathering, but a full celebration. Cupcakes, cookies, the kind of food you buy when you want the night to taste special: ceviche, carnitas, Dos XX, charcuteries trays and glass bottle Cokes. All my closest friends from the island came. Music and laughter filled the day and carried into the night.

I thought about flying out and attending the graduation ceremony in the U.S., but by then, I had already committed to pursuing my master's degree. I promised myself I would walk the stage for that one. This night was for now. Still, even among my friend and chosen family there was a quiet ache. None of my family from the States came. For a brief moment moment, imposter syndrome whispered again.

Somewhere deep in the corner of my mind, that familiar ache lingered. The absence of the people you were born and raised among. A quiet voice reminding me I might not belong anywhere completely. The same feeling I had in the hospital, not knowing if I would walk again, when none of my family of origin, my brothers, sisters, aunts, and uncles thought that I was not worth visiting, especially since if I died there would be a party after the funeral. But as I looked around my yard and house: Music loud and laughter swirling, their smiles and cheers washing over me.

This party and this celebration weren't just about a degree. It was about keeping a promise I had made years ago to the little girl. Again, to myself as a struggling single mother, unsure if I'd ever finish college. That promise had once felt fragile, like a distant hope. It was a promise stated all those years ago in high school, when I had spent my afternoons in community college. I carried it through detours, doubts, and long nights.

It was also a celebration of what a good support system can bring. My dear friend Capi was there with his family, of course. A couple of close gringo friends. The dog walker who helped me when Corona was young and would knock me down. So many people came and went that I truly lost count.

I caught the eye of *"The Carpintero."* He always made sure my home, patio, fences, and furniture were beautiful. Eventually, his actions, words and his presence have made me feel beautiful as well. He showed up in my life when I needed him, in his calm steady way that I learned so much from. Tonight, he was in the background letting me shine: Picking up plates, refilling *cubetas* (buckets) of beer, even making drinks to help out. As always, when he, Capi and I were together, we had to tell everyone the story of how Capi had introduced us 3 years earlier. I am happy that he became part of my life and cannot imagine a time he never will be. He grounds me.

These were my people: Friends who knew I would support them in whatever way they needed, and they would do the same for me.

That day was the start of another level in my life. One where I let myself believe that was enough.

And now, I'm working towards my master's in psychology at another online university. I've lived a thousand lives in one it seems.

But this one? This one is mine, the one I am Choosing to live.

I used to think my role was only to help others reach their dreams. I didn't believe mine mattered anymore. But I've learned something simple and sacred:

They do.

My dreams matter. My story matters. And it's never too late to claim what was always meant to be mine.

Epilogue: I Know a Girl

I Know a Girl:

I know the little girl version of myself that shadowed me for many years, trying to pull herself out of her past. Whispering to me: *Can we?* Standing beside me when we did. Trying to find her way. Helping me to find mine. Using me to live out her dreams.

I am that little girl with the big dreams of migrations, travel and safety.

I am also the woman who chooses how my life looks today.

I live in a 50-by-50-meter concrete-walled square piece of heaven carved out of the Cozumel rainforest jungle. *La Selva. El Bosque* The jungle. The forest. It is my *Castillo de Princesa*. By most people's standards, it isn't much. Most Americans would think I live in a shack without the necessities.

To me, it's everything. It's a place that doesn't demand performance or perfection. It doesn't ask me to be anything but myself. It lets me rest. It is ***home.***

My little house was never meant to be a home at all. It was supposed to be an office. A forgotten footnote to a business plan that never came to life. But instead, it became a sanctuary. Transformed into a studio house, tucked in the trees, surrounded by the kind of stillness you can't find in cities or schedules or to-do lists.

That little ignored house has become the foundation of a business plan I never dreamed I could have. I assist and coach others who have been through similar circumstances. I am the farthest thing ever from a counselor. My clients unpack their past with others: I am here to meet them where they are and help them improve their lives. Everything around me is a metaphor for my only life.

Peace, I've learned, and I also teach, is not something you fight for. It's something you surrender to.

Outside my window each morning, hummingbirds flit like tiny messengers from the universe, their wings a blur of soundless hymns. Butterflies rise like scattered prayers into the heat. Sometimes Monarchs pass through, reminding me of my childhood wonder. My plants, dozens of them, spill from their pots and stretch from the earth, seeking the sun through the trees, living examples of peace and harmony and growing to their full potential even on days when I cannot. Their flowers and leaf colors bloom and fade, and bloom again. Even plants know beauty, healing, growth and rest come in cycles.

I share this space with Corona, the stubborn little Mexican girl who got her name from the virus that brought the world to its knees. Corona was a castaway baby, unwanted, needy and desperate for love. My soul twin. She is fierce, funny, loyal to the bone. She is my protector from snakes, rats, tarantulas, and big fat toads. She has no fear and is a true assassin. She would go after the wild Javelinas if she could find a way over that 8-foot wall.

She, like me, also has a soft side. She is in love with every baby chicken she has ever met. She will lie in front of the brooder cage and just watch them with wonder. She doesn't care that I fall down from my old injuries when we take a walk together. She only cares that I get back up. She nudges me until I do. She jumps up on me in the middle of the night to curl up beside me in a hammock, just as she did as a baby.

She and I live with fat happy chickens who gift me the eggs I share with my little community of friends and my chosen family. We have a few roosters who wake us up every morning singing for the sun that another day deserves to break. Even on the days when my depression raises its demonic face, the sun comes up, the roosters still sing, and the eggs need to be gathered, and Corona paws me awake to go outside. I am no longer afraid to go to bed: No one is there to hurt me.

I live alone, but I am not alone every day. I have a maid and an caretaker for the yard that come often. They don't just care for my home and garden, they remind me that I still deserve dignity, even with disabilities, even in the days I struggle most. Being able to provide financially for two other families gives me another sense of purpose in life

I have people who love me. And who I love. *The Carpintero, Capi and his family, my maid, a few friends, Corona's babysitter,* and others have given me reason to believe that people really can love me, even with all my faults and doubts.

My CPTSD and my traumatic brain injury, souvenirs from the wreck that could have ended it all, have started to creep into more days than not. It settles over me like fog. Sometimes I forget where I was going, almost always forget what groceries to buy or if I have taken my medication. I lose the thread of my own words, both in English and in Spanish. I don't drive anymore. I order food more and more often because I forget to cook or burn it when I do. I am blessed that there is very little fast food on the island, "ordering in" is fresh tacos, tamal, birria, hamburgers and fried chicken, even fresh green garden salads and amazing fresh fruit plates.

A taxi driver that I have trusted for years gets me where I need to go, even if I can't always explain the way.

Some might call me dependent. An invalid, maybe. I call myself adaptable and stubborn.

I speak to my grown children over Facebook calls or the occasional phone call. Their lives are far from mine now. Geographically, emotionally, in what they care about and how they live. We still find ways to meet in the middle. And when I press that green button and hear their voices, I remember the hardest and best thing I ever accomplished. I raised them, and I kept all us alive. They may not have had the childhood of their dreams, but they are chasing and living their own dreams today. I have learned also, to stay out of their way and let them! They are capable and can achieve whatever they want! I am still able to help support the startup companies they have, and I am proud of them for their ventures.

I am not saying that life is perfect. I am saying that I am still trying. There is a mantra that I tell myself whenever I can remember...

I am Amy. And I will be okay.

I am not healed. I am healing.

I am not whole. But I am no longer shattered.

I am not what the world once told me I had to be.

I am who I am. And I know her now. I know her well.

I am the girl who was lost and still found her way home.

I am the girl who slept in shelters and still stood tall.

I am the girl who stared into the eyes of fear and said, "Not today."

I am the girl who learned to accept and give love.

I am the girl who came to Mexico to disappear—but ended up being found.

I am Amy.